Kevan Manwaring won the Bardic Chair of Caer Badon (Bath) in 1998 and became a professional storyteller in 2000. He is a founding member of Fire Springs and performs with his partner, Chantelle Smith, in the duo Bríghíd's Flame. He is the author of *The Bardic Handbook* (2006), *The Way of Awen: journey of a bard* (2010); *Desiring Dragons: creativity, imagination and the writer's quest* (2014); *Oxfordshire Folk Tales* (2012), *Northamptonshire Folk Tales* (2013), *Lost Islands: inventing Avalon, destroying Eden* (2010), the Windsmith Elegy fantasy series (2004–12), and over a dozen collections of poetry. He is the editor of *Ballad Tales* (2017) and blogs and tweets as the Bardic Academic.

Also by Kevan Manwaring:

fiction

The Long Woman
Windsmith
The Well Under the Sea
The Burning Path
This Fearful Tempest
Ballad Tales (editor)
Northamptonshire Folk Tales
Oxfordshire Folk Tales

non-fiction

Desiring Dragons
Turning the Wheel
The Way of Awen
The Book of the Bardic Chair
Lost Islands
The Bardic Handbook

poetry

Lost Border
The Immanent Moment
Green Fire
Waking the Night
Immrama
Spring Fall

Silver Branch

bardic poems

Kevan Manwaring

AWEN
Stroud

First published in 2018 by Awen Publications
12 Belle Vue Close, Stroud GL5 1ND, England
www.awenpublications.co.uk

Poems in this book were previously published in: *Remembrance Days* (self-published, 1991); *A Pennyworth of Elevation* (Imp Press, 1993); *British Poetry Review* (1993); *Gramarye* (Imp Press, 1994); *Spring Fall* (Imp Press, 1998); *Immrama* (Imp Press, 2000); *Generations*, ed. C. Williamson (Poetry Can, 2000); *Waking the Night* (Riverside Press, 2002); *Writing the Land* (Awen, 2003); *Green Fire* (Awen, 2004); *Dragon Dance* (Awen, 2005); *The Bardic Handbook* (Gothic Image, 2006); *Into the Further Reaches*, ed. Jay Ramsay (PS Avalon, 2007); *Thirteen Treasures* (Awen, 2008); *The William Blake Birthday Book*, ed. Felicity Roma Bowers (Bow of Burning Gold, 2007); *Wild Blood* (Away, 2009); *Avebury Moon* (Awen, 2010); *The Immanent Moment* (Awen, 2010, 2012, 2016); *The Way of Awen* (O Books, 2010); *Soul of the Earth*, ed. Jay Ramsay (Awen, 2011); *Lost Border* (Chrysalis, 2015).

Cover design: Kirsty Hartsiotis
Editing: Anthony Nanson
Proofreading: Richard Selby

ISBN 978-1-906900-42-7

For more information about Kevan Manwaring visit:
www.kevanmanwaring.co.uk

The Poet's Prayer
In silence can poetry be found,
at peace listen to the world's sound,
in stillness, sense its motion,
in humility offer devotion.
To honour creation,
make sacred the air ~
this is the poet's prayer.
KM'17

Thank you to all those who have encouraged, listened to and published my poems, and to Awen for letting me shake the silver branch.

Contents

Foreword

In an era that regards myth as an untruth, rather than as the truest thing of all, it takes courage to step into the ring and stand up for, or embody, the myths of a land. Kevan Manwaring dares to do that in this collection, calling upon the inspiration that brought us Taliesin, Blake and the many unknown poets who opened to us the hinterland of our native otherworld through their vision.

The bright knowledge of our druidic ancestors was laid down, not in writing, but in poetry, a bird that rested upon the bough of memory on the tree of tradition. Held in this memory were all the creatures, people, beings, places and events that shaped understanding. From this deeper history, we draw up our souls' inspiration still, and so it is that, in this collection, you will find its reflection and likeness, so that we do not forget the many-layered world of our origins. As the World Wide Web is to our own world, so the poetic memory was to our ancestors, where one metaphor might convey a raft of interwoven allusions. It is still true today, if you have the vision to read the land that you walk upon; if you have the ears to hear the stories upon the wind and waters; if you can perceive the ancestors who witness you and who look to your hands, feet and voices to act, dance and speak for the abiding spirit of the land.

Within *Silver Branch*, the ancient and modern worlds are woven together in the remaking with which we have to engage at every moment, perceiving the ancient and allowing its currency to irrigate our time and deepen our, often, surface culture. As ancestral structures fall away, as wise councils fall into argument and short-term decision-making, as the beauty of nature is despoiled, so it becomes our bounden duty to listen harder and deeper to the mythic levels of our collective life.

In ancient Ireland, all poets who had qualified as 'ollamhs' (the equivalent of our academic title of 'doctor') carried a silver branch: a branch with metal bells upon it that heralded the coming of a walking repository of memory. When the branch was shaken purposefully in an assembly, then the company fell silent, in order to not disturb the poet, but also to give honour to the tree of tradition and its fruits. Fall silent now and hear the voice of the bard!

Caitlín Matthews

Preface

This book brings together a quarter of a century of bardic endeavour. It shows a cross-section of my work from the very earliest poems to the most recent. Although I cannot claim that all were written with an intentionally 'bardic' consciousness (with a heightened sense of orality, aurality and mythopoeia), I can in hindsight discern evidence of that in all of the pieces included here. It seems to me they are all part of one continuous project, certainly they are all manifestations of what I have called the 'Way of Awen', and here in Gairloch Bay, on the far northwest coast of Scotland on writing retreat, I trust I am continuing down that bonnie road in my current projects.

I have written over a dozen collections of poetry – from my first crudely put-together effort (typed all in upper case, photocopied and stapled), to self-illustrated pamphlets, to perfect-bound digitally printed editions published by Awen and poems included in various anthologies. So, what to select?

I have decided to choose only those poems I have performed in public in a bardic manner (i.e. from memory) or that have a foregrounded oral quality that lends itself to recitation. Most fall into the first category.

I have found I can learn a poem by rote fairly quickly – usually within half an hour – but it takes a lot longer for it to become embodied and hardwired within me so that I can perform it without rehearsal at the drop of a hat. In such a way many of these poems have become longstanding, tried and trusted companions along the road – a mnemonic, internalised collection alongside my repertoire of stories and songs. I have woven them into storytelling gigs, stitched them into a folk circle, a gathering, protest, or ceremony. Having seen the success of these impromptu performances, I encourage readers to try doing the same. Practise at home. Maybe have a go at learning a poem by heart and then try it out on friends and family, strangers, even animals and whatever may be listening in the wild. I have found wildlife can be most responsive.

The bardic community is a circle whose circumference is nowhere and centre everywhere. It is wherever folk pass around the silver branch and share their awen. I hope this book will inspire you to be part of that. To assist in that aim I have included the full text of *Speak Like Rain: Letters to a Young Bard*, originally written as part of my master's in creative writing at Cardiff University and published as a chapbook by Awen in 2004. Its inclusion is intended not to be prescriptive, but to provide a primer in practical techniques of composition and performance for those who need it. Some readers will be experienced writers and performers and may read this merely out of curiosity, but others may be looking for inspiration or even initiation. If my *Silver Branch* encourages you to craft your own poems, to generate a repertoire of gramarye and to go forth and share it wherever the awen allows, then its fruit will have passed on their seed.

Kevan Manwaring

Speak Like Rain:

letters to a young bard

Introduction

This collection of seven letters was inspired by Rainer Maria Rilke's famous sequence to the young poet Franz Xaver Kappus.[1] Mine are addressed to a young performance poet I know well – myself, twelve years ago, when I began to write poetry in earnest. I had written one poem before this as an English exercise at school. But it wasn't until my gap year before college that the Muse truly came to me – or rather I found her, while hitchhiking around the West of Ireland in the summer of 1991. I had visited Thor Ballylee and Coole Park, Yeats's old haunts, and poetry was stirring within me, when I met a young lady in Kennedy Park in Galway on a scorching ice-cream-melting day. The encounter was brief, just one day together, talking, sharing dreams, but we stayed in touch. I sent her a poem our meeting had inspired, 'Circle Dance' – using the metaphor of the sun and moon only glimpsing each other at rare times. The idea was better than the finished piece. It was the first poem I had written for an audience, albeit of one. It was the beginning of a long lyrical correspondence and the start of my poetic career.

I focused on performance poetry, partly through a frustration about getting published, about getting the work 'out there', but mainly because I believed in the magic of the spoken word, the shamanic aspect of performance, and I became interested in the bardic tradition of the Celts. The bards were originally shamans who received messages from the Otherworld in a trance state, they found, in their reliance on memory, a natural ally to the art of poetry. What had come out of the visions in a torrent of words could more easily be remembered when patterned by metre and alliteration. So the craft of verse-making became intimately associated with magical practice and Otherworld power; and has remained so throughout Celtic history.[2]

My poetry began with a series of letters to Ireland and so it is apt to reflect upon my development since then in the same format. These letters are 'things I wish I knew then that I know now' about the craft of writing to perform. If I'd had the benefit of advice that someone twelve years more experienced in the field could have offered me, my learning curve would have been immensely faster. Instead, I was an autodidact, learning painfully through trial and error. Nothing can replace the value of experiential learning, but much time and embarrassment might have been saved with a few simple tips. I am not claiming to be the authority on the subject, but I certainly am the expert when it comes to myself, and these letters are pitched at someone I know inside out. I am not attempting to 'speak like Rainer' – just in his pedagogical spirit. I include quotations where appropriate, but the thrust of these letters is what twelve years of performing poetry has taught me.

The main 'lessons' are based on my Shining Word workshops, in which I teach the craft of writing to perform. Their title alludes to Taliesin of Welsh myth, whose name means 'Shining Brow'. The young Gwion Bach accidentally sips from the Cauldron of Inspiration and after a shape-shifting chase by the sorceress Ceridwen, he is 'twice-born' and becomes the master bard. John Matthews suggests that on one level Taliesin is 'An initiate shaman who, by submitting to the tests of the Cauldron, is made a fully-fledged practitioner of the shamanic arts.'[3]

Yet the story can also be interpreted as a the rites of passage of a poet, for that is what Taliesin indeed becomes. So I refer to my younger self as 'Gwion'. The initiated bardic poet (one who remembers and performs his words) becomes a 'Taliesin': like the 'Merlin', it is a title, a mantle of office, and there may have been more than one.

Here is revealed the method I use to manifest a performance poem. Although my words always begin on the page in some form, often the poem is not finalised on paper until it has been performed several times. For me, the performance is part of the craft of writing the poem. It feeds back into the finished piece. By exploring the whole cycle I offer an insight into my techniques of composition and revision. I have included a toolkit of techniques in the appendices.

Perhaps these 'letters from the future' will be of use to other fledgling bards. May they make fewer mistakes than me! They are written with the benefit of what Coleridge calls the 'lantern at the stern':

> If men could learn from history what lessons it might teach us. But passion and party blind our eyes, and the light which experience gives us is a lantern on the stern which shines only on the waves behind us.[4]

Composing these letters has helped me assess how far I have come and the extent of my knowledge (and ignorance). It has been an audit of knowledge and an ordering of thought. Learning is about assimilating and evaluating experience. If someone hands 'the truth' to you on a plate, it is often unpalatable. One has to come to it through cognitive processes. Yet, if good things are placed before us, occasionally a chord is struck, because it echoes something we have felt but been unable to articulate. We are halfway there already. This is the power of words that call to you, unlocking the dormant wisdom within:

> It comes through the written and spoken word; sometimes a word, a sentence or a poem or a story, is so resonant, so right, it causes us to remember, at least for an instant, what substance we are really made from and where is our true home.[5]

By writing these letters of the craft, I have defined the stuff that my poems are made of. I hope they inspire you to write and perform your own.

Notes

[1] Rainer Maria Rilke, *Letters to a Young Poet*, trans. Stephen Mitchell, Random House, New York, 1984.

[2] Alexei Kondratiev, *Celtic Rituals: An Authentic Guide to Ancient Celtic Spirituality*, New Celtic, 1999, p. 10.

[3] John Matthews, *Taliesin: The Last Celtic Shaman*, Inner Traditions, Rochester, 2002, pp. 14–18.

[4] Stanley Taylor Coleridge, *The Poetical Works*, Frederick Warne, London, 1921, p. 357.

[5] Clarissa Pinkola Estés, *Women Who Run with the Wolves*, Ebury Press, London, 1992, p. 7.

Letter 1

April Fool's Day, 2003

Dear Gwion,

It's been raining heavily and I am drenched, hair wet rat-tails, skin glistening, clothes damp, as I sit on the train home writing this. It's like someone's turned on the taps today, in two ways. Instant April showers, after weeks of unseasonal sunshine. And a break-through with my 'craft of writing' essay that I've worked on for a whole month. After ten thousand words and reaching saturation point, the waters have burst today – I had a brainstorm to write this hard-won advice to you, my younger self. To the fool I was then from the fool I am now, twelve years 'wiser'. Yet at thirty-three I claim to be no wise elder. All I can offer you is the benefit of my experience, the knowledge I have found in my studies, and point you in the right direction.

I know you don't like taking advice and you certainly don't like being told what to do, but for your own benefit I urge you to read on – if you want to become a better poet sooner. If you cannot listen to anyone else, listen to me.

Just think how you would have benefited from a visiting poet back at school. Although you enjoyed doing English Literature 'A' Level immensely, the poetry taught was generally grim (e.g. the War Poets) and generally dull (Poets of the Thirties) – light years removed from your reality. I knew it was good, and 'good for me', but only now am I beginning to fully enjoy reading some of it. It seemed you had to be dead to be a poet, and write about *serious* things.

No one told you poetry can be fun, poetry can be passionate, poetry can be like rock 'n' roll – that reading it out loud can give you a rush better than any drug, that performing it can be the most exhilarating experience.

Could you have imagined performing to thousands in Trafalgar Square a protest poem off the top of your head, unrehearsed, unexpected? Or being regularly on the bill at Glastonbury Festival? Being paid to perform and to run workshops? Winning the Bardic Chair of Bath? Or being flown to the States to recite? No? Well, all these things have happened to me in the decade or so since I dedicated myself to this path. I'm not saying that I'm rich or famous or have 'made it' – if you want to make money do something more practical – only that I've been successful in following the path of my heart (after many dead ends and diversions).

If you could have learnt how to perform poetry back in Mereway, it would have improved your self-esteem and communication skills immensely. You would have gained confidence, eloquence and enhanced self-image when you badly needed it. Instead it took you years.

With this in mind, I intend to share some of my experience on the subject of writing to perform poetry. It will be a workshop in letter form, with 'hand-outs' about techniques of writing and performing to demonstrate how I and others go about it. I will refer to people I have learnt from or admire. Those who know better than me.

By embarking upon this path, you are becoming part of a tradition, a tradition you must learn from and honour. Listen to the masters of the craft. Respect their wisdom. We walk in the footsteps of giants; they have made the way easier for us.

I know you want freedom in your performance poetry – to 'have the gag removed from one's mouth', as Walt Whitman says in 'One Hour of Madness and Joy'[1] – but the more adept you are, the clearer your voice will ring out. You can only do this by mastering the form. Don't be afraid to learn the traditional rules of poetry – it will only improve *your* poetry.

Sheer enthusiasm will only get you so far. Passion transcends ability, for sure, but you don't want to be writing doggerel, do you?

You want to be in control of what you write and how you sound. To do this you need to master the techniques and be fully conscious of everything that is happening in the poem. Ignorance is no excuse. You must learn the rules before you can break them. As Yeats said in 'Under Ben Bulben':

> Irish poets, learn your trade,
> Sing whatever is well made,
> Scorn the sort now growing up
> All out of shape from toe to top,
> Their unremembering hearts and heads
> Base-born products of base beds.[2]

You wouldn't want your poetry to be 'all out of shape' now, would you? Master the form, young man. Craft your words with loving care. Your effort will pay off.

Writing is one of the few things in life that does reciprocate the energy you put into it. It has been the one constant in my life, the one sure thing that I have been able to rely on through 'weal or woe'. It is your staff. It will help you live your truth by following the path of the heart. That is, of course, if you are serious about this, if you are willing to make the commitment. Robert Graves said in *The White Goddess*, 'I do not even know that you are serious in your poetic profession.'[3] Well, I know, with hindsight, that you are, but you still must rise to this challenge. Take your 'craft and sullen art'[4] seriously, as Dylan Thomas puts it, and others will begin to also. It is a labour of love. If you are willing to slave away at your words with little or no gain except the satisfaction that 'saying what you mean and meaning what you say' may bring – finding the precise phrase that expresses perfectly what you intend – then carry on.

The title of this series of letters I will send to you over the next six months comes from Isak Dinesen's description of the response of African Kikuyu boys to her sing-song nonsense poetry.[5] In traditional African life, rain is a welcome thing, it brings life, it refreshes and nourishes. This is what performance poetry can be like at its best, for both speaker and audience. To 'speak like rain' can be the best feeling in the world. It is a joy to do and it is a joy for others to hear. This is when the 'awen' (Welsh: 'inspiration') comes. As an 'awenyddion' (inspired one)[6] you become enthused ('en theos' – 'in God') and the divine (or higher self/power) speaks through you, like rain from heaven. The goal is to step out of the way as much as possible: 'I learned to get out of the way and let that creative force work through me.'[7]

In my letters I shall provide some ways of doing this. The letters are inspired by the German poet Rainer Maria Rilke's *Letters to a Young Poet*, that is, to Franz Xaver Kappus, who said of them, 'And when a great and singular voice speaks, the lesser have to keep quiet.'[8] I believe that the 'great and singular voice' is the higher self and the lesser include the ego; we have to put aside our petty concerns, kill the darlings, to let the genius of the poem emerge – the 'genius' being the spirit of the piece. We must strive, 'to seize the inmost form' like Blake,[9] and cut the wheat from the chaff. This is achieved through rigorous editing. We have to be our own worse critic. Find the critical voice before it finds you!

Yours in awen,
Tallyessin[10] /|\

Notes

[1] Walt Whitman, *Complete Poetry and Selected Prose*, ed. J.E. Miller, Riverside, Boston, 1959, pp.79–80.

[2] W.B. Yeats, *The Collected Poems*, Wordsworth, Ware, 1994, p. 303.

[3] Robert Graves, *The White Goddess*, Faber & Faber, London, 1961, p. 15.

[4] Dylan Thomas, *Omnibus: Poems, Stories & Broadcasts*, Phoenix, London, 2000, p. 91.

[5] D. Gioia & X.J. Kennedy (eds), *An Introduction to Poetry*, 9th edn, Longman, New York, 1997, p. 157.

[6] Matthews, *Taliesin*, p. 192.

[7] Julia Cameron, *The Artist's Way*, Pan Books, London, 1995, p. xiv.

[8] Rilke, *Letters to a Young Poet.*

[9] William Blake, *Complete Works*, Wordsworth, Ware, 1995, p. 126.

[10] I stopped using this stage name in 2007 but have retained it here to preserve the dialogic device.

Letter 2

Dear Gwion,

I am going to make you a star. A five-pointed star, to be precise. Like Gawain's shield pentagram, representing for him the five Christian virtues, this star represents five qualities I consider necessary for great performance poetry (see page 283). They are Breath, Passion, Compassion, Grounding and Silence and they relate to the four traditional elements – air, fire, water and earth – and the fifth element spirit. It is this we are to consider today, here, at the start of things.

In the beginning was the Word, but before the beginning there must have been Silence. I believe our job as poets, paradoxically, is to let the silence speak, as clearly as possible – between the gaps of our words. I call this the Endless Sound, identifiable with the Buddhist mantra A-U-M – the fourth unspoken syllable being Silence. It underpins everything else. It is the voice of the universe. We must learn to listen to it. What does it want us to say?

Before we speak we must learn to listen. This is the first lesson. We must sensitise ourselves to life, fine-tune our senses, become as clear a lens as possible, to receive every detail, every impression, every sensation, every emotion, as vividly as we can; then we are ready to write. This is my 'Poet's Prayer':

In silence can poetry be found,
At peace listen to the world's sound,
In stillness sense its motion,
In humility offer devotion.
To honour Creation,
Make sacred the air –
This is the poet's prayer.

We receive inspiration from spirit and we receive spirit in silence. Practise meditation in whatever form you find most suitable: sitting, chanting, walking, dancing, running – any repetitive action that bypasses the conscious brain. We want to access the subconscious, where the good stuff comes from – the stuff that dreams are made of. The strange associations found there will circumvent cliché, will outshine anything you can think of logically. As Rilke says to Kappus: 'Allow your judgments their own silent, undisturbed development, which, like all progress, must come from deep within and cannot be forced or hastened.'[1]

As with meditation, the harder you try to force inspiration, the less likely it is to happen. Yet there are plenty of exercises to loosen us up – for instance, hot-penning, the automatic writing of the Surrealists. Write for twenty minutes, without taking the pen off the page, anything that comes into your head: last night's dream, shopping lists, what you saw on telly, foolish fears, impossible notions – anything. Eventually, from the psychobabble, some pearls may emerge. But it doesn't matter if they don't. The exercise purely serves to download what's rattling around in your head, turn down that white noise, lessen the internal dialogue.

It is said that every twenty minutes there is a natural lull in conversation – a Hermes pause, presumably because the winged messenger needs a breather now and again! That is the silent moment when spirit speaks.

Julia Cameron has her own version of this exercise: 'morning pages'.[2] Three pages at the beginning of every day, failure on pain of death. Like literary ablutions, once they are done you are ready to work. And to make work your prayer. 'All work is empty save when there is love,' as Kahlil Gibran says in *The Prophet*.[3] 'And what is it to work with love?' he asks. 'It is to weave the cloth with threads drawn from your heart, even as if your beloved were to wear that cloth.'[4]

The Prophet Speaks of Prayer

I cannot teach you how to pray in words.
  God listens not to your words save when He
Himself utters them through your lips.
  And I cannot teach you the prayer of the seas
and the forests and the mountains.
  But you who are born of the mountains and
the forests and the seas can find their prayer in
your heart,
  And if you but listen in the stillness of the night
you shall hear them saying in silence.[5]

In performance poetry we are returning to something primal, to shamanic utterance, to gramarye, to word magic. You must use words responsibly, sensitively and imaginatively – return their meaning to people, or play on their meanings, by re-presenting them in unusual ways. And the power of your message is expressed just as forcibly by what is not said as by what is. The negative spaces between the words. Tell by absence. W.S. Merwin describes this brilliantly in 'The Child':

This silence coming at intervals out of the shell of names
It must be all of one person really coming at
Different hours for the same thing.[6]

So when we perform our poetry we must make room for the silence. It allows the audience to digest what they have just heard, allows room for them; otherwise you are in danger of blocking them out with a bombardment of words, projecting out and not letting them in. It is a dance between the two – you need to project, physically and psychically, but see this as a fisherman casting out his line. With your poem-bait, you want to reel them in. Hook your audience with eye contact, with your body language, tone of voice and rhetoric, but allow them enough slack to make their own connections. Give them space to breathe.

This leads on to our next letter-lesson – on air. Until then, keep listening.

Yours in awen,
Tallyessin /|\

Notes

[1] Rilke, *Letters to a Young Poet*, p. 1.

[2] Cameron, *The Artist's Way*, p. 9.

[3] Kahlil Gibran, *The Prophet*, Pan Books, London, 1980, p. 33.

[4] Ibid., p. 34.

[5] Ibid., p. 81

[6] Alan Jacobs (ed.), *The Element Book of Mystical Verse*, Element Books, Shaftesbury, 1997, p. 506.

Letter 3

Dear Gwion,

Let us take the air together. Breathe deep, fill your lungs, exhale. Feels good, doesn't it? In many cultures, breath is the essence of life – and some believe we had life breathed into us by a Creator. And we give our words life with breath. 'There is no better way to understand a poem than to effectively read it aloud.'[1]

In the magical tradition it is thought bad luck to blow a candle out, because you are 'killing' the flame with life – literally wasting your breath. We should be careful not to do this in a performance, for our words to be merely hot air, 'full of sound and fury, signifying nothing'.[2] You can avoid doing so by carefully crafting your words so they are the most economical and elegant you can make them. As William Blake says in 'The Crystal Cabinet', '[strive] to seize the inmost form'.[3] As in Michelangelo's block of marble, dormant within your rough-hewn first draft is the perfect form, your *David.*

Writing poetry you are sculpting sound. Basil Bunting suggests taking a 'chisel to write'.[4] Chip away the excess by constant redrafting. 'Hacking back' I call it. Yet, however brutal the process of composition and revision, the final piece should seem effortless and music to your ears. I find that through my speaking the poem over and over again the words fall into place and any burrs are smoothed out, until it scans to the ear.

At this stage do not worry how it looks on the page, except in suggesting pacing and stresses by lineation. It is this musicality that is primary in performance poetry. As T.S. Eliot says in his essay 'The Music of Poetry': 'the music of poetry is not something which exists apart from the meaning'.[5] Eliot is referring to page poetry, but this is common ground. As Pope once said: 'The Sound must seem an Echo to the Sense.'

Such onomatopoeia echoes back to what anthropologist Mircea Eliade calls 'participation mystique' – sympathetic magic. By knowing the name of a something you have power over it, and by naming it you conjure it in the air before the 'tribe', the audience. Speak with authority, but also wonder, as if you were saying each word for the first time. As if the words you have spoken you have only just thought of.

In *Zen in the Art of Archery* Eugen Herrigel offers a brilliant metaphor for life in the discipline of archery which can be applied to performance poetry. He says,

> Instead of reeling off the ceremony like something learned by heart, it will then be as if you were creating it under the inspiration of the moment, so that the dance and the dancer are one and the same.[6]

How do we re-access that inspiration? At this stage through breath. Controlled breathing, or awareness of breath, is a common technique in meditation. It circulates energy through your body, but also can open you up, via a kind of self-hypnosis, as can be induced by mantras, to heightened states of consciousness where you may receive wisdom. In the Welsh bardic tradition this is called 'awen', which means 'inspiration' or 'flowing spirit'.

> The old Irish word *uath*, 'poetic art', is clearly of archaic origin. *Awen*, its Welsh cognate, is linked, in a text quoted by Watkins, with *seis*, 'musical art', *cluas*, 'hearing', *anal*, 'breath'. Thus at least two of the primary senses, breath and hearing, are seen as forming an integral part in the experience of inspiration; the poet breathes in the awen, hears it and gives it forth in musical speech or song.[7]

We receive awen by asking for it, humbly, from the Muse. Bards call it down by intoning it three times, imagining its light entering the pineal gland of the third eye, opening up a channel between the brow and throat chakras, so that they speak with spirit.

This is an excellent way of warming up the voice before a performance, but it can be used whenever you want words to flow – on page or stage. It should be used as a respectful invocation of the Muse's blessing. I believe it's no coincidence that 'awen' sounds like 'amen'.

The Irish mystic A.E. (aka George Russell) wrote of what he called 'That Lordly Utterance' in *The Candle of Vision*:

> I look on the poet as prophet though too often they have not kept faith with the invisible … But at times they receive the oracles, as did the sibyls of old, because in the practice of their art they preserve the ancient tradition of inspiration and they wait for it with airy uplifted mind.[8]

So let us presume you have gained inspiration from the mountain peak of your imagination with an 'airy uplifted mind'. Now you have to capture that poem on paper: what I call 'mapping sound'.

Wordsworth famously described poetry as 'emotion recollected in tranquillity'. I suggest performance poetry is a *recreation* of that emotion. The moment is captured like a genie in a bottle, to be let out at each performance, to be lived again. A.E. suggests, 'The poem seemed like an oracle delivered to the waking self from some dweller or genie in the innermost.'[9]

Let's get technical for a minute. Ezra Pound suggests there are two sorts of poetry: 'Music … forcing itself into articulate speech' and 'Sculpture or painting forcing itself into words'.[10] He saw an axis of the aural imagination and an axis of the visual imagination. He breaks this down further into three categories: (1) 'melopoeia' – music; (2) 'phanopoeia' – visual; and (3) 'logopoeia' – meaning. It's interesting that J.R.R. Tolkien talked of what he termed 'mythopoeia'[11] – which I would consider the spirit of the piece, its mythic dimension and archetypal power. Coleridge defined the same three things as poetry of the ear, poetry of the eye and poetry of meaning.[12] Aristotle termed them 'melos', 'opsis' and 'lexis' and saw the first two as contributing to the third, i.e. meaning emerges from the sound and visual quality of a piece.[13]

We are concerned here primarily with the first category – poetry of the ear. This was the focus of Greek, Provençal and Celtic poetry – but not exclusively. We are dealing with Pound's 'language in colour', as Basil Bunting nails it: 'lines of sound drawn in the air',[14] or, as I like to put it, 'painting in sound'. I consider performance poetry a modern continuation of the oral tradition. It is about the spoken rather than written word, and if there is a text then it is the script for a performance – not a substitute for engaging with the audience. The performance exists in the negative space between poet, poem and audience. It is created in the moment, unique and transient. A sound mandala similar to the Buddhist sand mandalas, made with loving detail as an act of devotion, then swept away to remind all of the impermanence of existence and to defy the ego and commodification – that's the ethos of avant-garde performance art. The performance has brought the words alive and they will now resonate with the poet's voice in the memory of the listener.

Yet, live, a performance poem is only as good as its audience. The sentences are given sentience in their minds and imagination. They bring it alive and are as much participants in its creation as the poet – through their presence, reciprocity (full attention, heckling, or applause), receiving of sound, recreation of visual imagery in their imagination, and empathy.

I would define performance poetry, whether it begins life in a book or not, as 'the remembered and recited word', to distinguish it from conventional poetry *readings*. The latter have their place but do not concern us here. Although it is possible to give entertaining readings, these are the exception. So many poetry readings are dull because the work is not being performed – there is little or no awareness of audience or stage presence, of projection or microphone technique.

When a poem is performed it should become something else, in the same way a film adaptation of a novel should; otherwise what is the point? It should not simply be a cold reading aloud of the text. The listener cannot share in the delight of the printed word like a reader. You have to make it come alive with breath, feeling and energy, making 'feral poetry' as Australian poet Les Murray calls it. All the audience has to go on is the sound of your words and any visual qualities, so body language and eye contact help immensely. If the poet makes the effort to learn his or her poems off by heart, it improves the quality of the performance, and the audience appreciate the effort – they are impressed and you are on to a winner straight away.

In *By Heart* Ted Hughes describes different techniques for remembering poems.[15] At your age I never thought I could remember poems, having had no drama training. Yet through years of developing my memory muscles I have been able to perform whole shows without text, for instance, my nine-page cyberpunk version of *Beowulf*, 'Bio*Wolf' (see page 61). Having augmented my repertoire through storytelling over the last three years I now know about a hundred stories and poems by heart. Yet this pales in comparison with the graduate bards, who were expected to know 350 after twelve years training!

Do not be daunted by this. There are methods. Learning by rote is reliable but tedious. And there are other ways. Using images engages the imagination and creates links through a train of association. You break down the poem into key images – the more grotesque or absurd, the more memorable they are – and then, 'if each image is "photographed" mentally as on a screen, it will not be forgotten easily. And each image will bring on the next which has been connected to it.'[16]

You are never remembering more than one connection at a time: this makes it possible to learn long pieces. You just have to trust your memory to make that association. The more you practise, the more readily that link will snap into place.

However, 'In many people, the audial memory is much stronger than the visual. It is wide open to any distinct pattern of sounds.'[17] In verse, this pattern of sound is created by the 'interwoven texture of syllables',[18] the alternation of vowels and consonants, the rhythm and overall inflection. 'The stronger the pattern is, the more memorable the line will be.'[19] 'It roots itself directly in the nerves of the ear.'[20]

Other mnemonics too, such as *tried* and *trusted* alliteration, are good stalwarts – allies of the open mike that will not let you down. Your tongue slots into place at the beginning of each word, a kind of muscle memory akin to the musician's dexterity.

This is the great secret that Tristan Tzara reveals in Part 4 of the *Dadaist Manifesto* when he writes, 'Thought is made in the mouth.'[21] The flow of sound can suggest paths for the meaning to manifest – whatever rolls off the tongue, sometimes to our regret! Vicente Huidobro in Canto 1 of *Altazor* calls it 'the wind that's trapped in your voice'.[22] Each vowel provides a gate, each consonant a filter – like the logic pathways of a computer programme.

But do not forgot the metaphorical undercurrent of the poem. By constructing a poem with a mythic logic, a 'mythopoeic structure' if you like, an inner reality and consistency, you have a trusty guide through the linguistic maze. If it makes sense in your mind, it will make sense in your mouth, for 'the hidden patterns are … much the stronger'.[23] Combined, these qualities create an unforgettable poem, with its own dramatic impetus: 'We feel them almost as a physical momentum of inevitability, a current of syntactical force purposefully directed like the flight of an arrow in the dark.'[24]

Yet we must not let the poem take us over so completely we lose control – because this is when the performance deteriorates and becomes a rant. Always remember to breathe when performing poetry. It's easy to get swept along and become breathless. Then you start to stumble and slur, or find it difficult to finish a line or give it enough power because you've run out of steam. And let the poem breathe and speak for itself. Poems are your arrows – but let them find their own targets, by their own merits. Less is more, but don't undersell yourself; always reach beyond. The Zen master observed,

> Your arrows do not carry because they do not reach far enough spiritually. You must act as if the goal were infinitely far off. For the master teaches it a fact of common experience that a good archer can shoot further with a medium-strong

> bow than the unspiritual archer can with the strongest. It does not depend on the bow, but on the presence of mind, on the vitality and awareness with which you shoot. In order to unleash the full force of this spiritual awareness you must perform the ceremony differently: rather as a good dancer dances. If you do this, your movements will spring from the centre, from the seat of right breathing.[25]

So breathe your prayers and you shall speak with presence and eloquence. This can be achieved by following Bunting's advice to 'compose aloud – poetry is sound'. Train your ear to scan by becoming familiar with verse forms, with good poetry. Hone your palette by imbibing the finest you can find. Learn to listen to poems on a number of levels. Breathe in the best, until like a piano-tuner you can tell when something is off-key and know how to fine-tune it by adjusting the subtle internal tensions of the piece, tightening a metaphor here, trimming a line there.

Speak each phrase several times and let your tongue be your tuning fork:

> I want to rediscover the secret of great speech and of great burning. I want to say storm. I want to say river. I want to say tornado. I want to say leaf, I want to say tree. I want to be soaked by every rainfall, moistened by every dew. As frenetic blood rolls on the slow current of the eye, I want to roll words like maddened horse like new children like clotted milk like curfew like traces of a temple like precious stones buried deep enough to daunt all miners. The man who couldn't understand me couldn't understand the roaring of a tiger.[26]

Yours in awen,
Tallyessin /|\

Notes

[1] Gioia & Kennedy, *An Introduction to Poetry*, p. 174.

[2] William Shakespeare, *Macbeth*, Act V, scene v.

[3] Blake, *Complete Works*, p. 126.

[4] Basil Bunting, *Briggflats*, Fulcrum Press, London, 1966, lines 115–17.

[5] Gioia & Kennedy, *An Introduction to Poetry*, p. 178

[6] Eugen Herrigel, *Zen in the Art of Archery*, trans. R.F.C. Hull, Penguin Books, London, 1985, p. 78.

[7] Matthews, *Taliesin*, pp. 111–12.

[8] A.E., *Song and Its Fountains*, Macmillan, New York, 1932, p. 56.

[9] Ibid., p. 21.

[10] W.N. Herbert & M. Hollis (eds), *Strong Words*, Bloodaxe Books, Hexham, 2000, p. 15.

[11] J.R.R. Tolkien, *The Monsters and the Critics*, HarperCollins, London, 1997, pp. 109–61.

[12] Herbert & Hollis, *Strong Words*, pp. 17–25.

[13] See Northrop Frye, *Anatomy of Criticism: Four Essays*, Princeton University Press, Princeton, NJ.

[14] Herbert & Hollis, *Strong Words*, pp. 80–2.

[15] Ted Hughes (ed.), *By Heart: 101 Poems to Remember*, Faber & Faber, London, 1997.

[16] Ibid., p. xi.

[17] Ibid., p. xiii.

[18] Ibid.

[19] Ibid.

[20] Ibid., p. xiv.

[21] Tristan Tzara, 'Dadaist Manifesto', 1918.

[22] Quoted in J. Rothenberg, *Writing Through: Translations and Variations*, Wesleyan University Press, Middletown, CT, 2004, p. 56.

[23] Hughes, *By Heart*, p. xv.

[24] Ibid.

[25] Herrigel, *Zen in the Art of Archery*, pp. 77–8.

[26] Aime Cesaire, *Return to My Native Land*, trans. Berger & Bostock, Penguin Books, London, 1969.

Letter 4

Dear Gwion,

Let us now turn to the fire, to the passion of the piece. You have something burning in your breast – you want to share it, you want to light up the world with your vision. Let's face it, the world needs that. Clarissa Pinkola Estés writes,

> One of the most calming and powerful actions you can do to intervene in a stormy world is to stand up and show your soul. Soul on deck shines like gold in dark times. The light of the soul throws sparks, can send up flares, builds signal fires, causes proper matters to catch fire. To display the lantern of soul in shadowy times like these – to be fierce and to show mercy towards others, both, are acts of immense bravery and greatest necessity. Struggling souls catch light from other souls who are fully lit and willing to show it. If you would help to calm the tumult, this is one of the strongest things you can do.[1]

This resonates deeply in me and reminds me of a poem I wrote in 1999 called 'Candle Sun':

> In the loam of darkness
> plant a seed of light.

With spark Divine rekindle
Those whose glow falters.[2]

To shine in the darkness. To be truly, fully, yourself. The 'fire in the heart', as I call it (after Yeats's 'fire in the head'[3]), forces you to speak. But you must harness it, discipline it. You don't want to be a 'fire and brimstone' preacher – threatening your audience with hell-fire and damnation if they don't buck their ideas up. It has to be used in moderation. Like the young men taken off by the tribal shaman to be initiated into the mysteries of fire, you must learn to respect both the fire and those who carry it and pass it on.

Listen to any teachers you are lucky enough to come across. As Yann Martel says in his Booker Prize winning novel *Life of Pi*, 'It was my luck to have a few good teachers in my youth, men and women who came into my dark head and lit a match.'[4] They will inspire you and perhaps, perhaps, your words will inspire others.

In an ideal performance there is a transference of energy between the performer and the audience: 'a poem is energy transferred from where the poet got it … it is a high-energy construct and, at all points, an energy discharge'.[5]

James Fenton, poet and Oxford professor of poetry, talks of writing into the dark: 'When you are actually engaged in the process of writing you must always be writing into the dark.'[6] Although I think he was referring to the nebulous process of interacting with consciousness and the unconscious, I would like to take the statement more literally and propose as an alternative 'writing with the lights on': the idea that one should illuminate the process of writing as much as possible with self-reflection and critical appraisal, but also with an awareness of audience. Writing into the dark works fine as a method for composing page poetry, but for the stage the 'lights on' method is more appropriate. You may have a specific audience in mind if you know where a piece you're writing is going to be performed. Or you may select appropriate material or alter your delivery. But you have to be careful about 'playing to the crowd'. It is impossible to second guess an audience accurately. You don't want to be writing just what you think they want to hear. It has to come from the heart if it's going to be worth its salt.

The old man of the mountains, Chinese philosopher Lao Tzu, said,

Seek to find the core of your life-force
in the sacred flame of the soul.[7]

This is the energy of the piece and the chi of the performer. The former you want to trap inside the lamp of your poem, ready to be released at will. Use that breath to feed the flames. Walt Whitman in his ecstatic 'One Hour to Madness and Joy' asked,

What is this that frees me so in storms?
What do my shouts amid lightnings and raging winds mean?[8]

When performing you are in the eye of the storm. It is exhilarating and intoxicating – but be careful it doesn't make you tongue-tied or egotistical. A tight form will keep the energy under control – channelling it through metre, rhythm and rhyme – and a bit of humility will restrain the hubris. Remember the fates of Prometheus and Icarus – both punished for their audacity, as echoed in Blake's 'The Tiger': 'What, the hand dare seize the fire?'[9]

In 'Prophets of Los' – named after Blake's god of the imagination – I dare the poet 'to burn with a stolen fire'. In my 'Wicker Man' poem (see page 123), the poet himself is ablaze:

I am the Wicker Man, burning up inside,
hollow shell, nothing to hide.
I want to be the fuel of my own bonfire.
Let my life by my pyre.

Not to have lived fully
is the only death.
I want to burn brighter
with my every breath.
Leaves these wooden bones in a heap,
Like wild flames I want to leap.

This poem has two important qualities for performance poetry: *rhythm* and *strength*. Rhythm in a poem is like the rubbing of the fire-bow or the beating of a drum. The faster you go, the hotter it gets. Your words are kindling, you fan the flames with your breath and as the fire gets going it begins to suck it in – until you become breathless.

Lemn Sissay, whom I would call the Jimi Hendrix of performance poetry, is a maestro of this breath-rhythm, as in his high-octane rap with the chorus 'I've got the rhythm.' When he's in full flow he's like a human combustion engine – or should that be 'composition'? Internal composition.

In a radio interview Sissay talked about angry youths like him 'having miniature explosions in their heart'. He was angry at being adopted and deprived of his cultural inheritance until later in life. Does the 'storm that rages around your youthful head', as he put it, sound familiar? By putting it into words with rhythm and strength you can exorcise your demons and entertain.

One performance poet whose work exemplifies these qualities is Benjamin Zephaniah:

> Dis poetry is like a riddim dat drops
> de tongue fires a riddim that shoot like shots
> Dis poetry is designed fe rantin
> Dance hall style, Big Mouth chanting,
> Dis poetry nar put yu to sleep
> Preaching follow me
> Like yu is blind sheep,
> Dis poetry is not Party Political
> Not designed fe dose who are critical[10]

You want to be a lean, mean rhyming machine – no flab, just the gift of the gab. 'Cerdd dafod' is the Welsh name for poetry and literally means 'tongue [or mouth] music'. Dormant for centuries, this *verbal* quality was accentuated by some (Blake, Gerard Manley Hopkins, Yeats) but burst into full life again with the Beats. Charles Olson was their 'leading strategist and thinker'. He set out their unofficial manifesto in his seminal essay 'Projective Verse', where he talks of the performative qualities of poetry. He 'reconnected poetry to the body … For Olson, each line of poetry was both idiosyncratic and "necessary" as a result of a speaker's particular breath.'[11]

Your poems should be pared down to the bare essentials. Brevity is the soul of wit after all – to cut a long story short, to cut to the chase, to the quick, better read than dead. Your poem should be living, breathing, alert and street smart. It should be able to walk down the street with its head held high. You don't want a staring-at-your-shoes poem, a naval-gazing bedsit blues kind of poem. Never apologise for your work. Speak it loud and proud. Patience Agbabi is a diva of this kind of empowering performance poetry – full throttle, full-frontal, confrontational, yet controlled as a laser beam:

> Give me a stage and I'll cut form on it
> Give me a page and I'll perform on it.[12]

She successfully straddles the spoken and written word, untangling the conundrum of form and performance, as in her 'Seven Sisters' sequence of sestinas and the eponymous poem from her *Transformatrix* collection – a sonnet with attitude – which shows how traditional metric forms, many of them based on song forms, can aid performance when used imaginatively.

Be disciplined but never let anyone put out your fire. Shine and be true to yourself. Your integrity and vision will shine through. Blaze and be glorious. Enthusiasm is infectious (as is rhyming). Be bright, sparky, warm and good-humoured and people will gather around you. Where there's a hearth there's a performance space – wherever two or more are gathered in poetry's name … but don't bash people over the head with it. Don't force it on them, or forget to listen to them. As Lao Tzu said: 'Be bright but not blindingly so.'[13]

Be aware of your energy. Don't burn out. Raise your chi through warm-up exercises – then spend it wisely. It is the sacred breath. Blackwood and Skelton say,

> There are many verses, poems and songs, and even hymns, which could be labelled spells because they command a

change in the physical world, rather than intercede for it, or because they assert, or imply, the magical authority of either the speaker, or the spiritual powers of the natural world.[14]

A powerful example of this is by Hemans, a neglected nineteenth-century woman poet, in her evocation of 'The Druid Chorus on the Landing of the Romans':

By the dread and viewless powers
Whom the storms and seas obey,
From the Dark Isles mystic bowers,
Romans! o'er the deep away!

Think ye, 'tis but nature's gloom
O'er our shadowy coast which broods?
By the altar and the tomb,
Shun these haunted solitudes!

Know ye Mona's awful spells?
She the rolling orbs can stay!
She the mighty grave compels
Back to yield its fettered prey!

Fear ye not the lightning-stroke?
Mark ye not the fiery sky?
Hence! – around our central oak
Gods are gathering – Romans fly![15]

Rhetoric, repetition, alliteration, exclamation, an up-tempo rhyming scheme, like a quickening heartbeat – all contribute to the sound drama and make it very performable. Of course, this poem is written as direct speech and evokes the heightened emotion of the situation – the righteous anger of the persecuted.

In 'The Child of Everything' (see page 47) I adopted this defensive approach, creating a palisade of poetry to protect – in this instance – DNA, the essence of life, from being tinkered with by geneticists in GMOs (genetically modified organisms), one of the nightmares we today live with. I based the poem upon the incantatory ancient Irish 'Song of Amergin'. Here's the chorus:

I am the Child of Everything
do not play with my fire!
I defy your modifications
mutations not in isolation
their consequences will be dire …

My notion of the secret name of things could be seen as their DNA, their genetic blueprint. The African concept of 'nommo' – the magic name of things – I think relates to this. As does Adam's naming of the animals in Eden. By defining them, in a mythopoeic way he called them into being, in a similar way as Caedmon's angel bids him to 'Sing me the Creation'.[16]

I believe it is part of the poet's job to rediscover those lost names, or to invent new ones. Poetry operates within the secret language of words, revealing to the careful reader their inner workings, their quintessence.

Every poem saves a little bit more of life from extinction. As Roy Batty says in the climax of *Blade Runner*: 'All of this will be lost, like tears in the rain …' Unless it is captured by you in poetry and shared with art and heart. 'Because what should move people has to come from the heart,' writes Goethe in *Faust*.

Your words are the tinder – you want them to be as bone dry as possible. Avoid sogginess by cutting out the excess. Place them carefully together, a letter at a time, allowing them space to breathe, for the oxygen to get to them. Now strike a spark with your tongue and teeth, cradle it, caress it, blow on it and build it. Watch the flames rise higher and higher. Feed them with well-seasoned words. Enjoy the glow.

Give me a word
any word
let it roll across your tongue

like a dolly mixture.
Open your lips
say it loud
let each syllable vibrate
like a transistor.
Say it again again again again again
till it's a tongue twister
till its meaning is in tatters
till its meaning equals sound
now write it down[17]

Keep the fire.

Yours in awen,
Tallyessin /|\

Notes

[1] Clarissa Pinkola Estés, email circular, 10 April 2003.

[2] Kevan Manwaring, *Immrama*, Imp Press, Bath, 2000.

[3] Yeats, *The Collected Poems*, p. 47.

[4] Yann Martel, *Life of Pi*, Canongate, Edinburgh, 2003, p. 27.

[5] Charles Olson, 'Projective Verse', in *Postmodern American Poetry*, ed. P. Hoover, Norton, New York, 1994.

[6] Herbert & Hollis, *Strong Words*, p. 11.

[7] Lao Tzu, *Of Nourishment and Grace, Stillness and Compassion*, trans. Louisa Milne, Gaunts, 1996, p. 58.

[8] Whitman, *Complete Poetry and Selected Prose*, pp. 79–80.

[9] Blake, *Complete Works*, p. 71.

[10] Benjamin Zephaniah, quoted in Maria Damon, *Close Listening: Poetry and Performed Word*, W.E.B. Du Bois Institute, Cambridge, MA, p. 234.

[11] Olson, 'Projective Verse'.

[12] Patience Agbabi, *Transformatrix*, Canongate Books, Edinburgh, 2000, p. 11.

[13] Lao Tzu, *Of Nourishment and Grace*, p. 10.

14 R. Skelton & M. Blackwood (eds), *Earth, Air, Fire, Water*, Penguin Books, London, 1990, p. 5.

15 Felicia Hemans, *The Poetical Works of Mrs Hemans*, Henry Frowde, London, 1900, p. 120.

16 See Paul Matthews, *Sing Me the Creation: Creative Writing Sourcebook*, Hawthorn Press, Stroud, 2015.

17 Agbabi, *Transformatrix*, p. 9.

Letter 5

Dear Gwion,

After the fire, we need the water: passion must be balanced with compassion. To much hellfire and damnation and we are in danger of losing our audience, as Brian Patten captures amusingly in 'Spiritual Awareness':

> And when the doomy prophet says
> Yourejustavoidingtheissueyoupoorblindfools
> Yourejustavoidingthetrapsthepitsthechasms
> Theboilstheterribledarkawfulfuturethewaste
> Isunbelievablechildrenofsodomyoursmallsoul
> Isareinimmortaldangerandperilrepent
>
> Forgetting to mention a lot more,
> Let's just stretch out on the grass and smiling say
> OK for one day longer?[1]

After the breathless rant in the first stanza, the second comes as a relief. Most of the time, the general audience just wants to 'sit on the grass'; it doesn't want to be beaten over the head with your dogma. Don't proselytise. Just recreate that shining moment and let it speak for itself.

Imagine you are painting a watercolour. What kind of picture do you want to paint with your words? Each sound is a brushstroke. With delicate precision you build up the picture in the mind of the audience. Use silence like the watercolourist uses the white of the page. Every word matters. Let it have its space. Don't muddy the waters. The effect of each phrase is like dropping a pebble in a pond: you want its impact to be registered before you cast in the next one, otherwise you get interference.

Such cacophony can be used for effect when you want to jar people. Too much can be grating – unless that's your intended purpose, as in Adrian Mitchell's 'Autobahnmotorwayautoroute',[2] where phrases such as 'Citreonjaguarbugattivolksagenporschedaf' simulate bumper-to-bumper traffic jams, noise and visual pollution. Yet even in this poem there is the refrain 'slowly revolving', at one point in its own stanza, providing a contrast and suggesting the sluggish movement of the traffic. If you want something to stand out, then use a caesura or change of tack.

More usually, you should strive for euphony, for a lyric harmony. Being aware of the ripples in the pond means that though you can make them you should be able to control them – like a conductor with his orchestra. As I say in 'Canals of the Heart':

> Taking responsibility for the ripples we make.
> Leaving only shackles and goodwill in our wake.[3]

You want your words to flow. This can be achieved by making sure they scan, that you have removed all burrs. Then the awen flows like a stream over smoothed pebbles; your words have fallen into place, become rounded, solid. Think of your Green Man poem, 'One with the Land' – one of your first, which I still perform (see page 97). In fact, it has become something of an anthem. I have lost count of how many times I have performed it and I know it off pat:

I've been around since times began
and I may have lent a hand.
Y'see, my forte is creation,
making real what She has planned.

Your poem should provide the path of least resistance for your tongue. It should slide along with fluidic logic. Assonance and alliteration help: a similarity of sounds enable things to flow.

Yet most importantly: 'Karuna, Karuna' (the Buddhist concept of compassion quoted at the beginning of Aldous Huxley's *Island*[4]). No man is. You should have compassion for your audience and subject and yourself. After being sensitised for inspiration, you now need sensitivity to your surroundings.

There is a level of trust involved in listening – you are opening yourself up. You don't want to be screamed at. The performer must remember this. Respect your audience and they may respect you. Like the shaman, you may (ideally) be taking them on a healing journey. Your duty is to bring them back in one piece. This perhaps applies more to storytelling but there is an element of this with performance poetry.

A bittersweet example of this kind of healing journey can be found in London bard Francesca Beard's contemporary epic 'Photosynthesis'. It is almost Joycean in scope, but there is a sense of closure at the end, a kind of summarising and return to life with what we have learnt. This is the envoi – your farewell message. What do you want to leave the audience with? Despair, hope, indignation? Where have you arrived? What conclusions can be drawn, if any? Or do you choose a 'weak' ending, as opposed to a 'strong' one, an ambiguous tone suggesting a quantum uncertainty, or a symphonic resolution that hums in the brain?

There can be an electrifying quality in the best performance poetry or indeed any great art: meaning is found and value is restored to life (or the non-sense and ugliness are mirrored). This is akin to the elixir the hero returns with from his quest. He has journeyed into the otherworld and now returns with a healing vision for the tribe, as Parsifal, the holy fool, the 'freer of the waters', did by finally asking the Grail question of the suffering Fisher King: 'What ails thee, my Lord?'[5] And then the wounded king is healed and the Wasteland restored.

A powerful example of this is recorded in Gillian Clarke's 'Miracle on St David's Day', based upon a real experience she had in a care home where she was doing a reading. A perpetually silent patient was triggered by her poems to stand up and recite a whole speech learnt at school off by heart, surprising everyone there. Her words made the dumb speak.

If performance poetry has no other value, it at least enables people to have a voice. By crafting our words we are able to 'say what we mean and mean what we say' and then others are more prepared to listen. There is cathartic value in just getting something off your chest. Plenty of poetry readings seem to serve just that purpose – a kind of 'poets anonymous' support group. Survivors Poetry is specifically set up for this, and that is fine, but, ultimately, if you want people to listen for long then you really need to talk about something other than yourself.

I try to write about more universal subjects, although a particular experience may trigger a poem. The personal may act as a metaphor, but in performance poetry my gaze is always turned outwards – as in much Gaelic poetry, which often uses the landscape as a cipher. Derrik Thomson writes, 'Gaelic poetry, broadly speaking, is not strangely introspective … Even if he puts his verse to therapeutic uses he must not opt out of society.'[6]

You must accept responsibility for your words. Use them to heal, reveal and honour.

I was asked to write 'The Wheel of the Rose' (see page 84) for two friends getting married in a Scottish castle. It was performed during the ceremony in front of about a hundred people. The poem's rhyming couplets are an excellent mnemonic and were chosen to emulate union – hence a marriage of form and content.

I advocate poetry from the heart. Sure, sometimes it is necessary to write words that hurt, as in political satire, but there is too much suffering in the world as it is, so why create more? Better to create beauty, I think – old-fashioned as this may seem. Call me a modern romantic if you like. Anything but the death-by-irony of postmodernism, please!

Sincerity shines out. If you are willing to stand up there and speak your truth, from the heart, then people will listen. Of course, without art, they won't listen for long, so the key is to combine both. Art with heart. Use your gifts to help others to shine. Share the treasures you find. Sanctify with your words. Bless, heal and give hope. For the ripples you make will return to you threefold.

Yours in awen,
Tallyessin /|\

Notes

[1] B. Patten, *The Mersey Sound*, rev. edn, Penguin Books, London, 1983, p. 58.

[2] Seamus Heaney & Ted Hughes (eds), *The Rattle Bag*, Faber & Faber, London, p. 52.

[3] Kevan Manwaring, *Immrama*, Imp Press, Bath, 2000, p. 35.

[4] Aldous Huxley, *Island*, Chatto & Windus, London, 1962.

[5] Lindsay Clarke, *Parsifal*, HarperCollins, London, p. 204.

[6] Derrik Thomson, *Introduction to Gaelic Poetry*, Edinburgh University Press, Edinburgh, 1989, p. 88.

Letter 6

Dear Gwion,

Now it is time to ground our vision in structured verse. You want a good house for your awen to inhabit, made with love and solid lines. As Gibran says: 'build a house with affection, even as if your beloved were to dwell in that house'.[1]

Whether you use open or closed form, that is, free verse or traditional forms, there is no excuse for poor workmanship. Even if the poem is purely to be performed, full awareness of what the words are doing is essential. The piece must be disciplined and rigorously edited. The best place to do this is on the page before it is performed. Compose by the ear, for sure, but edit by the eye. Maybe subject it to the cold hard light of a workshop. Others can see faults that you will be blind to. And you will have little critical distance unless you've left the piece for a month or so. I write several drafts before I get it right.

We have baptised the poem in each of the elements; the final rite of passage is through earth. After the arc of inspiration, it is necessary to earth the current, to manifest it through a polished draught, rehearsal and performance. Time to get practical.

Firstly, what form will the poem inhabit? If you must use rhyme – it is an excellent mnemonic – then do so with the utmost caution. It is easy to slip into the ABAB quatrains of the ballads – the most popular folk verse form. Such songs use rhyme in a rough and ready way – fine if you have music to compensate and complement. But with naked verse you cannot afford to be so slipshod. Notice how abysmal many pop lyrics look on the page without music. You only have the spoken word – unless you want to get gimmicky with multimedia. Your job is to make your words as superb as possible.

The use of traditional verse form, with full or slant rhyming, is fine – if you can make it scan and manage to deploy inventive rhymes that surprise, subvert or sublimate the expectation of the line. Lazy rhyme schemes may make people nod off – rhyming couplets have an especially lullaby quality – but more unfamiliar ones (e.g. terza rima) will credit their intelligence and make them pay attention.

If you have to use any kind of rhyming, then make sure it scans! If you use an irregular rhythm, do so consciously and carefully. Traditional forms provide elegant rhyme schemes with established metres. The work is done for you. Why reinvent the wheel? When you have learnt the rules, then you can bend or break them – with awareness, skill, and invention. In his seminal work on story structure, *Story*, Robert McKee says, 'Anxious, inexperienced writers obey rules; rebellious unschooled writers break rules; an artist masters the form.'[2]

My personal preference is to let the poem find its own form. Sometimes it may rhyme; sometimes it doesn't. I like to play with the expectations of the ear, with assonance and dissonance, establishing patterns, then breaking them to make things stand out.

I believe poems have an innate music and it is the poet's task to find it and fine-tune his or her words until the poem sings. Some aspiring poets seem tone deaf – they have the idea, they can perhaps put it into words, technically it may even be proficient, but the poem is flat and out of tune. A 'piano-tuner', such as a creative writing teacher, can help you fix it, but isn't it better to develop the ear yourself?

Elizabeth Barrett Browning conveys this musicality superbly in 'A Musical Instrument':

> 'This is the way,' laughed the great god Pan.
> (Laughed while he sate by the river.)
> 'The only way, since gods began
> To make sweet music, they could succeed.'

Then, dropping his mouth to a hole in the reed,
he blew in power by the river.

Sweet, sweet, sweet, O Pan!
Piercing sweet by the river!
Blinding sweet, O great god Pan!
The sun on the hill forgot to die,
And the lilies revived, and the dragon-fly
Came back to dream on the river.[3]

If you choose 'composition by field'[4] then you really need as wide a palette of poetry techniques as possible at your disposal – not to use them all, like a child with a crayon box, but to be selective as an artist, discerning in the effects you employ.

Having created your masterpiece, how do you best bring it alive in performance? Well, through the five elements – to make a fully rounded piece. Let the poem perform you. Recite it over and over again and you'll find your body starting to move in rhythm to it, body language develop, expression and feeling emerge.

Watch yourself in a full-length mirror. Record yourself on video if possible; cringe-worthy as it seems, it is invaluable to noticing any personal blind spots: bad repetitive postures, any tics of gesture or voice. Iron these out – not to stop being yourself, but so you can use them consciously.

You have laboured long and hard over your words. Why screw it up with a sloppy performance? Edit yourself. Revise until your performance is the 'best version'. Of course, the performance varies each time and so it should – that is the beauty of live performance – but you want to achieve a certain plateau of quality before you go public.

Which brings me to my final point: awareness of venue. This is where your performance poem comes 'down to earth' – in this physical space. Walk around it beforehand, sense the energy of the place, its genius loci – and respond to this in your performance, express it even. If it's a festival, then get into the swing of things.

You want to synchronise with your audience; you want to be on their wavelength, or at least have a good idea what that is. Just before you perform, gauge the atmosphere. This is crucial. Alter your set if necessary. Don't be oblivious of what state of mind the audience is in – otherwise you are likely to get heckled, or die on stage.

Once, I performed a poem about 9/11 (a major tragedy that I wish I could warn you about, but the laws of causality prevent me) at the end of an open-mike cabaret night in a pub. The crowd was merry – it was nearly last orders. I hadn't expected to go on, but my friend offered me some of his slot. So on I want with my doom-and-gloom rant. It brought the house down, for sure – but not in the way I intended. Tumbleweed city … I managed to silence a whole drunken pub, but it was insensitivity on my part to kill the bonhomie like that. Be warned!

Use the space – the stage or performance area. Make the most of the physicality of your surroundings, using stage furniture as impromptu props. Make the stage yours. Don't stand in the corner, apologetic for your presence. This is not the time to be a wallflower. Stand up there and be counted. Be confident. In control. As Lao Tzu would say: 'Husband your space and power.'[5]

If you have to use a microphone, then make sure you know how to use it. Is it at the right height and angle? Is there feedback? Is it switched on? Don't shout, but don't stand too far away. Speak into it, but be careful with the plosives of 'p's. If possible, practise beforehand – do a sound check. Otherwise, ask the audience how you sound: 'Can you hear me at the back?' This is even more essential if you are performing without PA.

Learn how to project: breathe from the diaphragm so as not to strain your throat, and fill the room with your voice. Direct it like an *arrow of sound.* Pick people out of the audience to target key phrases at. Make eye contact with as many of them as possible. Always direct your words at them, otherwise the dramatic force of what you are saying is lost. Reach out to the audience with gesture and tone of voice. Draw them in – don't bombard them.

The Celtic god of eloquence, Ogma – father of the ogham alphabet – was said to have chains running from his tongue to the ears of his listeners. You want your audience to be equally hooked. In the Welsh story of 'Branwen Daughter of Llŷr' from the *Mabinogion*, the

Company of the Blessed Head listen enchanted to the severed oracular head of their fallen leader, mighty Bran, for eighty years without ageing, within a chambered room on an island, forgetting all of their grief. Entertained by their chief, as if he was his former self, they lost track of time until one of their number opened the forbidden door, out of curiosity, and the spell of the blessed head was broken. All that had befallen them returned in grim detail, and they had to return to the real world.

Let your words create such a sanctuary, holding the audience enchanted until it is time to go home. As Taliesin says in his bardic lore:

> Whoever shall hear my bardic books
> Shall obtain sanctuary in the Otherworld.[6]

I call this stage of the poetic process 'bringing the word home'. You have travelled through the elements and received their gifts. Now it is time to shine.

Stay in touch.

Yours in awen,
Tallyessin /|\

Notes

1 Gibran, *The Prophet*, p. 34.

2 Robert McKee, *Story: Substance, Structure, Style, and the Principles of Screenwriting*, Methuen, London, p. 3.

3 Hughes, *By Heart*, pp. 135–6.

4 As propounded by Charles Olsen in his 1948 manifesto 'Projective Verse', which advocated an approach to poetic composition informed by the 'propulsive force' of the poem and the actuality of breath, resulting in a transference of energy from the poet, through the poem, to the listener.

5 Lao Tzu, *Of Nourishment and Grace*, p. 36.

6 Matthews, *Taliesin*, p. 128.

Letter 7

Dear Gwion,

I have taught you five points I consider important for performance poetry (Air, Fire, Water, Earth, Spirit). Implement them all and your words will shine. A light will seem to pour out of you as you perform, as if you were on fire with spirit. This I call the 'Taliesin Effect': 'Behold the Radiant Brow!'[1]

When I started to work with the master bard, Taliesin Penbeirdd, I found my performance transformed: I became more fluid, as if mirroring the metamorphoses he went through. His creation myth was the first story I told unscripted at a party – and it was a success. After that, I identified strongly with him; he became a projected higher self. By 'channelling' him, I became a more confident performer. I believe confidence is like an overcoat, or cloak. It can be put on as and when necessary. I was never a natural performer – it is something I have learnt to do. I put on an act. I become that 'self-assured extrovert'. I learnt to craft my words so people would listen. The stage persona is a useful vehicle. One has to be careful, though, once this ego-construct has been created, that it does not get out of hand. Remember your humility and sense of humour. Don't take yourself too seriously. Always strive to let the words come through you, not from you. Know the limits of your knowledge. And know when to shut up.

Yet if you listen to the silence, make sacred the air, speak with fire, free the waters and bring your words back home, then the star will glow upon your brow and you will truly shine.

After the hours, days, months, even years of hard work comes the reflected glory of the finished piece. As Aime Cesaire chants in variants throughout *Return to My Native Land*: 'At the end of these small hours, my virile prayer.'[2]

What wins over an audience more than anything is a performer's 'energy' – their attitude, charisma and personal vitality. This is what people ultimately respond to. If you have this then you can say almost anything, because the audience is in the palm of your hand. You can see this with successful performers who have merely to pull a face, or say a stock phrase, to get a good response. They have an infectious personality. The audience get high on their energy, have a good laugh or cry and feel better. They are spellbound.

This relates back to the shamanic origins of performance. The medicine man or woman performs their healing dance and song for their patient, but the whole tribe benefits.

So always be aware of what it is you are actually doing. Jay Ramsay, in his 1985 manifesto *Psychic Poetry*, pinpoints this when he says, 'see through poems, see their value as energy, as signal, as depths of reaching: the poem means light, it means to release meaning back into life'.[3]

Come from the heart. Craft your words until they crackle. Create beauty by speaking your truth. Celebrate your existence and those around you.

In *Julius Caesar*, Shakespeare's Antony famously says, 'Lend me your ears.' We need to write performance poetry with the ears of the audience – imagining how it will be for them, hearing it as if for the first time. And when performing we must always remember to listen – to our words, to the silences and to the audience. And finally to feedback.

Rilke said to Kappus, 'No one can advise or help you – no one.'[4] I have to disagree with the maestro on this point. Although his advice was to 'go into yourself', it is always advisable to get your work read by others before going public. When you have immersed yourself in something so deeply, you lose your critical distance and begin to develop blind spots. Get it critiqued by the best you can find. But

I would wholeheartedly say that no on can tell you what to write. No one. Some may try – out of altruism or their own agendas. Heed Blake's 'Words of Los':

> I must Create a System, or be enslav'd by another Man's;
> I will not Reason and Compare: my business is to Create.[5]

Etch this with acid into your life. If you do not dream hard enough you will end up living in someone else's dream. Creative writing is one of the few freedoms we have left – yet even this can be controlled. Write to express your true nature, to defend what you believe passionately in. Do it well enough and you may inspire others to pick up the torch. Your goal is not to convert everybody to the 'one truth' but just to speak your own grain of it. To nail your colours to the mast. Even if it is in the midst of a storm. Indeed it is essential to stand your ground when beset by those who would test your beliefs, as Mandelstam points out so well in 'Last Poems':

> If our antagonists take me
> And people stop talking with me;
> If they confiscate the whole world –
> The right to breathe & open doors
> And affirm that existence will exist
> And that the people, like a judge, will judge;
> If they dare to keep me like an animal
> And fling my food on the floor –
> I won't fall silent or deaden the agony,
> But will write what I am free to write,
> And yoking ten oxen to my voice
> Will move my hand in the darkness like a plough
> And fall with the full heaviness of the harvest.[6]

Write what you are free to write, then yoke those 'ten oxen' to your voice and speak with power. If you do what you do with integrity and courage no one can hold a candle to you – you are being true to yourself. As hoary-headed Polonius says to Laertes: 'This above all, – to thine own self be true.'[7] Never try to please others by being false to who you are. The truth will out. Strive for emotional honesty in all your dealings with the world. The poet's grail is to express the truth of life – the raw quick of existence. Let your words be like Parsifal's lance and 'pierce through the middle'.[8]

All of life is a learning experience. Never stop asking the questions. Recognise the people who cross your path as teachers. See their light and let them see yours; never hide it under a bushel. Remember: she or he who does not shine will never be a star.

I am finding the best way to learn is to teach. You never stop learning – and the older I get the more I discover I don't know. Gone are the certainties of youth – the arrogance of ignoring those who have been before you. Let them guide your way though they cannot choose it. Learn from them all you can. Out of respect comes respect. Write out of consideration for your audience, be gentle but truthful with them and give freely of yourself.

Let the thunderheads descend, the bright bolt fall, and speak like rain.

Yours in awen,
Tallyessin /|\

Notes

[1] Matthews, *Taliesin*, p. 16.

[2] Cesaire, *Return to My Native Land.*

[3] Jay Ramsay, *Psychic Poetry: A Manifesto*, Diamond Press, London, 1985, pp. 10–71.

[4] Rilke, *Letters to a Young Poet*, p. 1.

[5] Blake, *Complete Works*, p. 293.

[6] Jerome Rothenberg & Pierre Joris (eds), *Poems for the Millennium*, University of California Press, Oakland, 2000, p. 396.

[7] *Hamlet*, Act 1, Scene iv.

[8] Clarke, *Parsifal*, p. 24.

Early Poems

Blessings of the Silver Branch

Bright salutations to this merry company,
high blessings to our generous host,
and peace to the spirits of this place.

I am Tallyessin the Bard
of Caer Badon, Caer Abiri and Côr Gawr,
and I come to you in this hall, at this hour.

I wield the silver branch,
ancient sign of my craft,
wise key to the Otherworld.

As the Queen of Elfhame's bell-strewn rein,
Aeneas's bough, the Apple Tree of Emain,
may it guide you there and back again.

Come with me and taste the apples of awen.
One bite will bestow wisdom and inspiration,
like three drops from the cauldron of Ceridwen.

Memory of animals be mine,
wisdom of ancestors be mine.
In the name of the God and the Goddess,
grant me your grace – let the brow shine!

I Am, My Dear Mary

I am, my dear Mary,
    a man born of a woman
    with but a short time
    to live;
    a bluebell that droops its head
    at the fickle spring light –
    nurtured from the turf
    and, in one swoop,
    felled,
    death after birth.

A poet is borne (in Her womb)
    and not mad.
    Two lived here – blind love birds:
    one strong, one weak, both at bliss.
    But one had hunger,
    the other was hungry.
    Greed cast them out too soon:
    the clumsy hand snatching for eggs.
    The sickly hatched;
    the bonny cracked.

There is one (still) born every minute.
    The waukly walked
    and soon he sang
    with a joyous voice.
    Rites of poesy made him free.
    Yet even the lofty lark
    has muddied claws
    and must eat the worms
    with those who fly
    not so high.

The mud that sticks carries far,
scattering seeds
plucked from the soil.
Wheat may come
that some will reap,
making bread
that some will eat.
They take off the crust
according to taste
and leave him not a crumb.

Although gorged on life's delights,
at a bitter cost,
his noble dome
could not be filled,
though he rimed his way
to its utmost hill –
joining stars by his lines,
turning over each new leaf
in search of something lost.

The green man turned grey
shattered by the clock of clay.
Her face, framed in fields,
furrowed unfamiliar.
Her eyes, summer wheels,
rolled by indifferent carts.
Her hand, he never held again,
until they both let go of life.
She gave him his first kiss of breath
and took his very last.

Alas! The man whose world was marred
by fences long and tall,
but the woman born of him
lived the longest of them all.

The Bard's Prayer

I can count the stars backwards
catch moonbeams in my pockets
tiptoe betwixt blades of grass
hear the crack of dawn
gild my eyelids with silver linings
skate the rainbow with golden shoes
drink a fairy's tears gathered in my navel
converse with grasshoppers by clicking my toes
breathe in so hard that my hair is sucked back
pick up footprints by retracing steps
leapfrog over low clouds
drink a stream dry
remember the name of every grain of sand
predict the path of shooting stars
make a ploughman's lunch with lunar cheese
sculpt the air with toothpicks
meet myself coming back before I get there
wish myself into tomorrow
and outrun my shadow
so
please believe me when I say

I am but a man of my word.

The Child of Everything

I am the Child of Everything
do not play with my fire!
I defy your modifications
mutations not in isolation
their consequences will be dire …

I am as old as creation
I am the genius of Genesis
I am the seed of paradise
I am the dancing serpent-twin
I am the fruit of knowledge
I am the sap of the world tree
I am the pulse of the planet's heart
I am in everything under the sun

I am the Child of Everything
do not play with my fire!
I defy your modifications
mutations not in isolation
their consequences will be dire …

I am the grit in the oyster
I am the gleam in your ancestor's eye
I am the quick of the dead
I am the dew on the divine web
I am the spawn in the gene pool
I am the fingerprints of parents
I am the pollen on the breeze
I am the eye of the storm

I am the Child of Everything
do not play with my fire!

I defy your modifications
mutations not in isolation
their consequences will be dire …

Thirty

I was born within a month of the moon-
landing and Woodstock,
coming down to Earth in a Midlands town.
Grew up feeling alien,
branded one of the X Generation.

Living in a hangover of Love,
getting shafted by the Seventies.
The power cuts, the Carpenters, the kitsch –
don't tell me it was cool.
Elvis obesity, Silver greed Jubilee,
But a Doctor knew
when the Force was with you.
Until anarchy in the UKA.
Every dog had its day
when Mrs T got in Number Ten
and the sentence began for the X Generation.

ZX81 to 1984, C5, Betamax, DeLorean car.
Why did I come of age in the Black Decade
that began with imagination's assassination?
A fashion massacre by clones in mascara,
mediocre music redeemed by Live Aid.
We saved the whale and ran the world,
watched Royal Wedding *Challenger* Tunnel,

played Space Invaders and Falklanders
when war was made to win elections.

Despite the solidarity of pit strikers and silo women,
Britannia was still going down on Ronald's Raygun.
But Frankie said Relax,
Just Say No, On Your Bike!
Pacman politics, living in a Rubics,
consuming in the shadow of the Apocalypse.
Midnight Watchmen waiting for the end:
did not foresee it would be the Berlin Wall.
The spies came in from the cold
and Mandela took a walk on the whiteside.
But the acid fell like rain from Chernobyl
and so we raved undercover,
ecstasy lovers,
dancing away the Recession and AIDS –
sweating out our Road Rage
in the Palace of the New Age.

Searching for the Beach …
Generation X Generation X

Yet that wasn't the be all and end all
of the Fin de Siècle.

Some of us took Direct Action in Faslane Polynesia and Seattle
Twyford Newbury Solsbury Swampy
CFC CJB BNP JCB
Crop circles Tiananmen Square Poll Tax Riots J18
Hunt Sab Animal Lab Reclaim the Gene
Butterfly fractals Desert Storm
Gaia exposed Global Warm
Big Mac Mad Cows
Genome GMOs
G8 Bill Gates

Murdoch
WTO
!

Now the WWWorld can know,
it's online but running out of time —
we are up to speed and in our prime.
Generation X Generation X.

Escaping the Matrix,
Dead End Dome.
Killing the Millennium –
living in the future.com

Generation X Generation X.

Rising from yesterday's shadow,
mutating tomorrow.
I'm texting about my gnrtn –
what's going to be your legacy?

Generation X Generation Y.

Keep asking the right questions
and don't let them steal your identity.
We can turn things around again –

Just give me thirty, give me thirty …

Phone Tree

I went for a walk in a yew wood
because a wire was in my head.
I tried to lose myself;
I lost my phone instead.
Disconnected, voxless, vexed,
unable to get an oral fix –
all that evening I sat in dumb gloom.

Did I still exist if no one was there to hear me –
like a tree falling alone –
unless eavesdropped upon by my mobile phone?
And did it make a sound
if no one was around?

What if the hundredth squirrel answered?
Would the caller be alarmed by bodiless barks?
By creakings and snappings?
By the hiss of shivering leaves?
By the rustling of unseen sylvans?
By the laughter of elves?
Would they hear the dryads singing?
Would they hear the world speak
and what would it say?

I retraced my absent-minded tramp
the following day
and found my erstwhile mobile
hiding in plain sight.

Relieved and annoyed
in equal measure,
I gave it a good talking to.

Bitterly I realised
that I could not live
without it.
I was a slave and the satellite
would always find me –

another disabled
on mobile dependency.

Roaming Home

I dreamt I roamed the South China Sea –
explored some of its endless mystery –
but now I'm roaming home, roaming home …

Started my journey with Siddhartha;
bummed around with Buddha;
jived with Jesus Presley of the Philippines;
and danced with Shiva on Huxley's island;
yet Mama Earth has the holiest shrines I've seen.

Alas, so many flock to Mammon's temples; the sky-rapers of
the capitals – raised for raising ringgit, baht, Singapore dollar,
peso, rupiah, Brunei dollar, Hong Kong dollar, US dollar –
dollar US, it's all so dolorous.

There were times when I shook death by the hand,
when my life depended on the roll of a dice:
and my soul seemed like a grain of sand
in this nightmare paradise, nightmare paradise.

Yes, the South China Sea!
I lived to tell you about its lunacy –
what a carnival of mortal folly.
Only the genius of Hesse, Gibran, Maugham and Conrad
stopped me from losing the thread.
And the words of a loved one,
like a cool breeze, the shadows of trees,
when you're under the sun, under the sun.

Sure, I've been exposed
to the passion of those Filipinos,
the acumen of the Chinese,
the tigerheart of the Tamil,
and those countless curious Indonese –
but there's no disease like families.

Blood is thicker than
the beautiful beleaguered South China Seas.

I may have drunk Mekhong whiskey
by the Mekhong river,
had strange folk sing me a familiar song,
but the camaraderie I discovered
does not make you belong.

So long to be where you belong.

I've wandered around the South China Sea
but though you're never alone it can be lonely.
O, this planet is so lonely.

So now I'm roaming home, roaming home –
getting nostalgic about the exotic …

When I kayaked into the serpent's lair,
trekked through screaming moon-forest,

ran the gauntlet of subterranean river,
the growling cave of death's nest.

I have tasted the bliss of the precipice!

To fly with psychedelic fish,
shower in a jungle waterfall,
be caught in a tropical squall,
navigate by Oriental stars
and stretch on dawn mountain
thin shadow far …
Around the South China Sea –
sometimes directed by serendipity,
though you should not leave it all to chance,
unless you want to be taken on a Devilish dance.

I've been shaken on so many rides,
to some far out places,
and if my luck had let me down
I wouldn't be seeing your faces.
Travelled in tuktuks, becaks, jeepney, jet ski,
horse-powered calesa, and seven-forty-seven.
And though none of the above would get you to Heaven,
that does not mean I wouldn't mind trying again.

With skull I have kissed the Equator
and by the skin of my teeth
climbed through the clouds,
to the summit of South East Asia,
but eventually you have to come down –
awake from the crazy phantasia.

Across the globe I have flown,
yet there's nothing quite like
flowing home, flowing home to
where my seed was sown …

I was dying to return from the South China Sea,
where there's just too much
fertility and fatality,
misery and brutality,
poverty and piracy,
ugliness and insanity,
illiteracy and litter in the sea.

Still my mind
is ablaze with the fire in my eyes –
what I've seen description defies …
tribal festivals and magical ceremonies,
water buffalo crawling to church on their knees,
plateaux and volcanoes,
parades and picture shows and
myriad human storms I've looked in the eye.

Yet only a few friends make amends
for the cruelty of humankind.
Otherwise you're on your own,
no face like home,
losing it in a crowd:
the world is so loud!
You can't hear yourself think,
can't breathe because of the stink, the stickiness, the fumes –
no respite, even in your rooms.
The bedbugs will bite all through the night
and when you're feverish you'll wish
you had not been so rash.

Do you really want to step out of the frying pan?
To have your ego shredded, bowels gutted, paradigm shifted?
To come back with no beach bum tan, merely weight loss,
and perhaps some truth plucked
from the bosom of chaos …

I have been around the South China Sea.

So

do these things only mean something to me?

Where on Earth do *you* want to be?
Out there?
Out there you won't find anything
that you can't already find within.

No matter how far you go you will always have
to face your fear.
So before you let go
of everything you hold dear

bear this in mind:

There's nowhere like home.
There is no *where* like home.

Know *here* like home,
Know *here* like home.

It is the only way to roam.

The Ruin

Well-wrought the wall –
Wyrd broke it.
Wyrd this stronghold burst.
Snapped roof-beams, felled towers.
The work of stonesmith giants moulders.
Rime scours gatepost and mortar,
shattered the shower-shields,
the heavy eaves.
Age under-ate them.

And the wielders and wrights?

Gone, long gone:
held fast in graves' grasp while fifty fathers and sons have passed.

Kings rose and fell.
Limestone wall once stood.
Now grey-lichened, arch-crashed –
standing still –
weapon-hacked, grim-ground.

Once shone the ancient skill sunk to loam-crust.

When God quickened mind
a man of wit,
cunning in rings,
bound the wall-base in iron –
a wonder!
Bright were the buildings,
halls where springs ran,
high, horn-gabled,
overflowing with the noise of the throng.

These mead halls men filled with loud wassail.

Wyrd changed that.

Death fetched off the flower of the people.
Where they stood and parleyed –
wasteplaces.
And on the temple precinct –
rubble.

Hosts who would build again toppled to the earth.

Therefore are these mosaic courts dreary.

Where terracotta tiles from roof-ridge fall
shatter

once many a man,
mood-glad,
gold-bright,
flushed with wine-pride,
flashing war-gear,
gazed on gleaming amber,
on shapely silver,
upon wealth held
and hoarded.

In this bold burg of broad dominion
stood stone houses
where streams swelled,
steaming from source,
and a wall caught all in its golden bosom
so that baths were hot at halls' hearth.

Fit for a king –
This city,
the ruin.

Roebuck in a Thicket

Through the darkening wood walking,
searching for signs of spring,
rain shadowed the brow of Solsbury,
wind worried the bare beech crowns.
Heavy air wearied me, my limbs warm lead.

Pausing on the black path,
I leant upon an elder,
small yet firm enough to be my staff.
The wrinkled bark chaffed the whorls of my fingers;
buds broke the twig tips.

Before me
a startled deer stood up,
a buck of sapling tines,
proud in coat of winter.

Freezing,
holding breath
amid bronchial branches,
he did not bolt, bold heart.

I tried to tell him I meant no harm,
that I was not the enemy.
Herne, did you hear?

In the twilight the moment dilated.
We stared in mirrored enchantment.

He began to walk towards me.
Reality buckled a little,

but out pact with nature is broken —

The deer thought better of it
and bounded away into the maze,
antlers amongst the trees.

The rain came on his heels,
pattering on the dead leaves.
I let go of the young elder,
feeling the sap quicken within.

Restored
by a draught of the wild,
I returned to my garden flat,
the roebuck to his thicket.

Bio*Wolf

Let us remember the Rebeginning …

It was the Year ZeroZeroZero
and the world had failed to end.
So humanity clicked on to a new K –
partying like there was no yesterday.
Time was their new God
and so, of course, they had to kill him.
Then they celebrated the anniversary of his death
every day for a year.

To hold this hyperparty
the ultimate venue was created.
On the Meridian
did *LaborTory*
a Pleasure Dome lottery.
Like the distended belly of a pregnant woman
it bloomed.
Inside, the Millennites were sustained umbilically
by hooka-pipes of protein
and comforted by the amneosis of chemical stimulants.
The only rule was

EVERYBODY MUST HAVE FUN.

Not dancing was forbidden.
All wallflowers were eradicated by ecstacide.
The CDJs were jacked into their skulls:

audio-implants were de rigueur.
Euphoria was regulated with the climate and lighting.
The atmosphere was truly electric.

Yet even without the fear of cold and hunger
the fun could not last for ever.
After nearly a year in this Palace of Excess
the Domers were zoned out.
In their ambient cocoons
they lay in serotonin depletion.

And that is when *Grendel* struck.

The 3D defences of the Dome were flawed:
they did not protect it from the fourth.
Through that space ran the Meridian line –
the Gatecrasher came through that gash in time.
Like a loving virus, he penetrated the firewall.
Into that immaculate mall he issued,
bringing his unfiltered filth and earthstench.
Bristling Mandelbrots,
multitusked,
Grendel caught the ravellers unawares
in their virtual haze.
Plugged into the latest CDreams
they orgasmed on the realism of the violence
as they were devoured.
Grendel gorged on the consumers,
massacred the techno-masochists.
Bloodgloss added vivid paint FX to the sensewalls.

In a trail of partygoer the beast departed.
Their revels now were ended.

… Morning and the trauma
services dealt with the aftermath

while survivors relived
their ordeals for the voyeur channels.
The scene of the slaughter was sealed off
until armoured forces manoeuvred into position.
Red alert they waited for the monster's return,
but when he came *Grendel* shrugged off their ambush – slaying
LaborTory's finest.
The victor of this cruel contest,
the Devil-from-Down-Below,
became the Lord of the Dome.
The UnderGod usurper
corrupted the architecture.
Lightning creepers
broke the designer lines.
His spore littered the dance floor.
Insects glistened on the carnage caused.
Grendel made himself at home in his charnel house.

Yet the government would not concede
to these chthonic forces,
the flies in their investment.
They called upon the special friendship they had
with a superpower …

In Gateland
a hero was engineered
to exorcise the ghost from their machine.
With humanity's genomes mapped
the Biotechnicians of *Sanmondo*
could select and enhance all the qualities they needed
for their genetically modified warrior.
The *Cybermensch* was born fully armed,
his body his weapon.
His codename *Bio**Wolf*.
With exoskeleton gleaming
and steroid muscles sculpted

to the proportions of a demigod
he was the paragon of progress.

From Gateland he came,
skimming hemisphere in stratoshuttle,
outrunning timezones,
homing in on the Dome,
the Millennium Crown
that had become a millstone to *LaborTory*.

An international holoday was declared
so that everyone could watch the live broadcast
of the greatest showdown the world had paid to view.
Lucrative contracts were signed
for exclusive coverage
and primetime advertising.
With hooked eyes the encouched public waited
as *Bio*Wolf* baited the dread Dome
with himself.

At the crack of dusk the nightspawn came.
With several tongues he licked his several lips
at the prospect of a fresh victim.
Yet this food was too fast.
*Bio*Wolf* gave him a taste of his own butchery.
As they clashed
commentators gushed,
wrestling with metaphors.
It was a battle of giants!

With a dash and a forward slash
Grendel tried to download his opponent
but *Bio*Wolf* backspaced and shifted,
seizing the monstrous claw thrust at him.
His adversary had never known such a grip.
Skin ripped, tendons snapped –

he was not hardwired –
and *Bio*Wolf* tore off the offending limb.
In agony *Grendel* lashed out with his one good arm,
catapulting his limb-axe into a gravity pool,
giving him time to escape – dripping his poisonous sap
and sloughing scales like crashing pixels …

The Dome was purged –
*Bio*Wolf* was victorious!
The nation roared for their eugenic gladiator
and in executive offices
champagne was popped
as deals were clinched
for VR games and action figures,
junk food and sportswear.
And the bells rang out across the tills of the land …

Grendel never haunted that hall again,
although there remained a grim memento of his passing.
His monstrous arm was displayed in formaldehyde –
*Bio*Wolf's* battle trophy for all to see.
Housed in the Fleshzone,
it made a fresh killing
for the reopened Dome.
Millions flocked to this museum of horror
and everyone wanted to meet its saviour.
*Bio*Wolf* became the flavour of the media's mouth.
He was a virtual phenomenon –
the man of the millennium!

Yet while the Biowarrior basked in glory
the slaughter recommenced –
with a vengeance.
Ghoulish visitors became the next victims
of that hellish clan.
This time there came a species more deadlier than man:

Grendel's blood-mother.
In her maternal wrath she wreacked havoc,
claiming eye for eye and tooth for tooth.
Satisfied blood-price had been paid,
she left through the rift she had made.

*Bio*Wolf* was confronted with a chorus of outrage.
Had he been too eager for acclaim –
having not finished the job?

To cries for an inquiry
his PR office cancelled all interviews
and in a desperate act of damage limitation
he went back to work.

The She-Beast was not hard to track:
*Bio*Wolf* followed her through the temporal crack …
The fissure spat him out at a black lake,
scum-ridden and foetid,
dominated by the genetic mills of *Sanmondo.*
Adjusting to subaquatic mode,
into the slimy darkness he dived.
Down, down into the icy depths he descended.
There, amid the dumped waste-flasks
he spied a sickly glow
and gleaned a banshee keening.

*Bio*Wolf* stormed the demons' lair,
ready for anything –
except a mother mourning her son.
She wailed for *Grendel* limp in her arms.
When she saw her child's murderer she screeched:
'*You! How dare you come here!*
Have you not done enough damage?
Are we not damned enough?!'

He tried not to listen
but her harsh words were inside his head.

'Why so cruel to your own kind?

'He was your prototype – a reject.
Your brother …

'And I am your mother!'
For an infinite moment
he was paralysed with disgust.
Was the mutant hag trying to kiss him?
No – scratch off his face.

As he was scarred
he unsheathed cybersword
and cut off her head.

Holding roots,
he hauled the mother load
back to the greasy surface –
blood thickening the water behind him …
With exoskeleton tarnished
and synthi-flesh torn
the haggard soldier returned through the fault
to the world's scrutiny.

Yet his victory redeemed him.
*Bio*Wolf* was hailed a hero once more.
No one knew what had transpired in that polluted mire.
He buried his dark deed
with the knowledge that gnawed at him.
His mother's head was interred in the Dome's white mount
for all to ogle,
until it mysteriously vanished –
back to Hell?

As Gateland's guardian
he maintained its multinational domain,
sustaining the consensus reality
for half a century.

Peace ruled.

The Gene Wars had been won.
The few remaining rebels had been obliterated –
their organic outposts purified by defoliant.
Beyond the UV deserts
the GMOzones flourished.
Famine was a thing of the past.

Unfortunately for humanity so was fertility.

Terminator seeds had infiltrated the food chain,
rendering mankind impotent.
With the population at 13 billion
Mother Earth breathed a sigh of relief.
The last generation lived on and on …
without the shadow of cancer, AIDS or age;
free from flaws,
with designer looks and IQ.
The High Breeds led erudite but bored lives,
their toil taken care of by mutant slaves –
the genetic underclass
whose parents had not been able to afford the right genes.

It was an Eden for some.

Only their dark angel's RAM dreams were disturbed
by nightmares of the Black Lake and its legacy.
Yet he had nothing to fear from his family loom.
Until,

as every podling now knows,
*Bio*Wolf* finally met his doom.

Fifty years on
the Dome had been demolished
so the Meridian could be raided
for the treasures of time …
And a dragon had been unleashed –
a leviathan more lethal than its kin.
It seemed to know the *Cybermensch*'s every move.

Not surprising considering its origin.
Sanmondo had decided it shrewd
to take their prodigy out
before he blew the whistle
in his outmoded dementia.
Through the softnet
they had monitored his nightmares.
It was time for their seed's termination
and so they had designed an assassin.

Ignorantly noble, *Bio*Wolf* leapt
to his land's defence,
donning the stagnant mantle for the last time.
He was glad for this call to arms
but the entropy had taken its toll.
Although not human his lot was mortal:
that which he cherished was to be his downfall.

Yet befitting a hero his death was glorious …
Systems failing,
engulfed in a plume of chemicalflame,
he dragged the dragon down into the Black Lake.

And this time he accepted
its fatal embrace …

Into the seething waters he melted,
back to his corrupt source.
Sanmondo's project was now liquidated:
their guinea pig could finally find peace.

Upon the site of the Dome
a mausoleum was raised
and down through the centuries his memory was praised –
until the conspiracy came to light.

Cyber cyber burning bright …

Spring Fall

the story of Sulis and Bladud of Bath

Sulis:

Pilgrims, pray listen to the Goddess speak:
as Sulis I flow through this Oracle.
Myriads now my healing waters seek,
finding not the secrets to my Temple.

To its subtle locks I possess the keys –
for I am the pure maiden of the Springs.
Illuminator of the Mysteries:
I, Priestess, Prophetess, Maker of Kings.

These misty waters are my scrying bowl –
ancient Mendip rain heated far below,
rising steaming to sky – as solar souls
always from winter's womb to summer grow.

It was in midnight days the vision came,
of a shining man – part-snake, part-winged –
who would found a golden city of fame …
Bath: remember your father, bright Bladud.

Bladud:

Raise not head – the day begins without sun.
For Hudibras Spearkeeper is sonless.
Bladud, his first and last born, he does shun.
No leprous heir for the house of Brutus.

This wood is now my home, my hearth hoar frost.
Outcast Prince Royal is now Prince of Swine …
Their breakfast on beechmast forgot – now lost!
Where they flew in this fog I must divine.

Through this black marsh their trail I can follow …
Glad sign, snowdrop – harbinger of spring.
There are my herd – in the mire they wallow!
Why, yes – the mud to their scurf is healing.

Perhaps their bath shall be my salvation.
Come, Greek scholar – a humble lesson learn.
Dear Goddess, these waters have their own sun!
Wise friends, for this warm balm we shall return …

Sulis:

Return he did, my Prince, every day.
Finding within my hot spring his poultice.
Until strong enough to go on his way,
'Always to remember,' was his promise.

So with a spring in his step off he set,
Swineherd no more – now fit for a kingdom.
Along the way impressing all he met
on flowering road to Trinovantum.

Finally, when day and night were equal,
Hudibras welcomed home his healed offspring.

'Forgive me, son,' said father prodigal.
'The land has an heir – let the minstrels sing!'

Soon the fading father the son outshone.
'Duty done. Time for a fitter steward.'
Thus Albion's old guardian passed beyond.
'Lud is dead!' they cried. 'Long live King Bladud!'

Bladud:

Good people – now has summer come with May.
This dawn I am torc-crowned your High King.
I declare this always your Holy Day.
Friends, mourn no more – let there be rejoicing!

Last night upon hills we leapt the Bel-Fire;
chased lovers who in the greenwood bedded;
made merry to make the crops grow higher …
Today it's to the land I am wedded.

Blessed Goddess, accept my solemn word:
with my life I'll love you and guard your wealth.
By Oak, my oath all here gathered have heard.
You I shall serve as long as I have health.

For my wondrous healing let the bards praise.
My first act is to fulfil a promise:
at her Springs I decree a temple raised,
so all may take the waters of Sulis.

Sulis:

To height of summer did High King ascend,
in majesty and sovereignty shine.
From the misty alder-moor he did render
in thanks and for the greater good my shrine.

With marble and limestone a dome to raise
to equal any form of Athens' fame.
Inside to symbolise spring's secret blaze,
King Bladud kindled an eternal flame.

Priestesses arrived to tend the Temple;
pilgrims poured for healing and augury
to the New Delphi with its Oracle –
whilst Bladud sought his own fate on Solsbury.

Seeking vision he climbed to the sky,
finding in his shadow a child without fear,
'A Goddess given son!' Bladud did cry.
'Now give me his name.' And the gulls cried,
'Lear!'

Bladud:

Goddess, now are days grown long and golden.
By your bounty are King and country blessed.
To sky have crops reached – like my Caer Badon.
Time to reap what is sown: to start harvest.

In valley I set a shrine to Sulis;
on hill established a city solar.
To this land brought the glories of Greece:
where I soared wishing others to venture.

The first university I began,
where the Four Paths Greek savants came to teach
to untap the vast potential of man –
for Divine Wisdom is not beyond reach.

With such wings of spirit we can aspire.
Is our mortal lot to toil, breed and die?

Not if man has more than mundane desire …
For the fruits of the Otherworld I fly!

Sulis:

So we reach the sunset of the Great Year,
when the weakening King did fiery wane –
his heels dogged by the new Prince Royal, Lear:
shadow growing of father's golden reign.

The crops had been gathered, the apples pressed.
The Sun King's seed had produced a good yield.
After fruitful graft it was time for rest –
only the Kingdom's head was not fulfilled.

Bladud's bright vision had made folk afraid.
His once-wonders were now necromancy.
The price for soaring high had to be paid.
His crime: showing them what Gods they could be.

To the music of the spheres all can dance –
until it is time to drink the dark wine.
Back to your Sulis – redress the balance.
Beloved, come embrace this earth of mine …

Bladud:

Albion, now is the time of the slaughter.
Samhain is here: take stock and salt your meat.
With wisdom make ready for the winter.
And my work is done with Great Year complete.

Here – in mighty temple of Apollo –
I end my span as the land's guardian.
Fiery at dusk falls my golden arrow …
Life, rain – my blood shall be my libation.

For my health restored and my life inspired
Sulis has my gratitude eternally.
To honour this debt cut off my head
and place it facing the Springs at Solsbury.

Now this heavy crown I hand to dear son.
The veil thins – I travel the road ancestral …
Light pyre – this flesh returns to the cauldron.
With feathered fire I am set free. Farewell!

Sulis:

Thus noble Bladud rose and fell –
his fortune fixed to Great Wheel.
Burning more than mortal candle …
for within is Flame Eternal.

The Solace of Sulis

Weary traveller
find sanctuary near.
Leave the false flow behind –
take a walk down Bridewell Lane
to the threshold of the White Doorway.

Enter with gentle feet –
for here life flowers from the cracked earth.
Hush and hark the magic gush.
Watch the wise waters rise
that fell as rain a hundred centuries ago …

As though the ancient thoughts
of a dormant giant,
bubbles aspire to the air,
steam dreams ascend
                                        to a sky of wings.

Scry the swirling mist: see what manifests …

Gaze into the eyes of the Goddess:
deep green pools wherein dwells
arcane knowledge;
bountiful fertility;
immortal beauty.

To the triple fountainhead of
Crone Mother Maiden
place your offerings.

Rekindle the temple flame
and honour She-with-a-Thousand-Names

who heals and inspires
with her sacred cauldron.

Deae Suli
Blessed Be

Awakening the King

Within the Spiral Castle
the sleeping King awaits,
awaits the Grail of the Fool …

On the Axis of the Starry Wheel,
inside the Glassy Citadel,
at the Head of the Winding Stairs,
the Head of the Winding Stairs.

He Dreams
upon a bed of broken wings –
an Icarus sunset, he fell
(and so must surely rise again).

Bright King awaken within.

From a gleam in the eye of night
to a star on the brow of day –
rise and shine,
spark to pyre,
pentagram, man,
breath to fire!

Phoenix,
return to the ashes of thy Resurrection.
To the Sacred Spring
where once you bathed as leprous swineherd
to emerge a king.

Bright King awaken within.

Angel of Bath, I invoke thee.
Many-feathered Man-God, I know thy name:
Bladud.

Bladud: father of Lear, son of Hudibras –
descended from Trojan Aeneas.
Bladud: temple-builder, necromancer –
raise thyself from the dead.
Bladud: magician, mathematician –
teach us thy wisdom.

Bladud: Arch-Druid, oak amongst men –
open thy seer eyes,
shake the snakes from thy hair,
stretch mighty limbs,
spread mended wings,
and soar

down to us souls,
to restore that which restored you –
the Shrine of Sulis.

Bright King awaken within.

Green Fire

Pagan Creed

I am a Pagan;
I belong to the world.
I am a Pagan,
Gaia's love child.
I am a Pagan;
Green Man stirs my blood.
I am a Pagan,
worshipping the wildwood.

The Earth is my temple;
the planet it is sacred.
I honour what sustains me;
by the feast of life I'm fed.

For those who've gone before,
and those yet to be,
let's leave this world better,
fertile, safe and free.

The two-legged, four-legged,
feathered, finned and furred,
from tiniest to mightiest –
may they all be heard.

In my magic harming none,
so let me work my will,
walking paths by other names,
we can be brothers still.

By the seasons of the sun
and the cycles of the moon,
by starlight, twilight and dawn,
by sigil, ogham and rune.

I take my vow,
never break my vow,
that Heaven is here and now!

Heathen, Wiccan, Druid, Priests High –
all Pagans under one sky.

I am a Pagan;
by spiral paths I roam.
I am a Pagan,
finally coming home.

I am Pagan;
find me by my star –
coven, moot, grove and clan,
the Gods know who you are!

The Bride of Spring

In darkest hour of the year
she arises

casting off her shadowy gown
as she steps over the horizon –
by sun king kissed,
borne by his golden down.

A dress of frosted cobwebs
veils maiden skin.
Within a season's turning
the crone has become virgin.

Snowdrops touch her
and turn into flowers
as the slumbering land stirs
in these formative hours.

The earth softens at her feet
where buds shake free their winter bed.
Newborn lambs begin to bleat –
insistent mouths by ewes' milk fed.

Rooster heralds her on the ground;
above, the feathered chorus
make naked trees resound.

We awake to a changing world –
her white magic revealed,
a petal uncurled.
Stone-bound man,
let your proud bells ring,

for we are welcomed into her garden
as she stand at the gates of spring.

The infant year she presents,
placing the future in our hands.
A gift of renewed innocence,

restoring the egg timer sands …

The Wheel of the Rose

From the ocean of the heart let Venus rise –
see her dawning in your lover's eyes.
In sighing chest she cannot hide –
flow to the rhythm of her tide.

Follow her seasons about the Earth;
who weathers them all will prove their worth.
Through weal and woe true love learns –
thus the wheel of the rose turns.

Who can say when love begins?
It is a circle that always spins –
around and around it our lives rotate.
Repeating the past is often our fate.

The arrows of Eros will be your thorn
until you worship Aphrodite's throne.
Offer yourself: mind, body and soul,
and she will heal you and make you whole.

Water this rose with the dew of your tears
and it will blossom all of your years.
Share this chalice with humanity,
and your life will be filled with harmony.

Blessed Is the Mother

Blessed is the Mother –
honour her on your day of birth.
Sacred is the Mother
whose body is this precious Earth.

Find her in the bend of a brook,
in the song of a secret spring.
Feel her in a verdant vale,
in the joy of nature's flowering.

Follow her contours in the curved breast of a mound,
in the swollen belly of a hill.
Face her in the fertile tomb of barrow womb,
in the dark and silence and still.

Madre Tierra, Prima Mater.

Earth Warriors, rise up!
Defend your Motherland.
The Dogs of Babylon
bite her fair hand.

Mothers of the Future,
may your hearts be true –
tomorrow's generation
all depends on you.

Blessed is the Mother
of all Creation great and small –
planet, animal, man and God:
the Mother Universal!

Madre Tierra, Prima Mater.
Madre Tierra, Prima Mater.

Birds of Rhiannon

From a high hill
you can see her coming –
riding along the bridal ways.
Wife of the Underworld
astride a white mare
and veiled in gold.

Try as you may
you will not catch her –
unless she wants to catch you.
The reins of your heart
are in her hands –
she's a wild wind from distant lands.

Hear the Birds of Rhiannon;
under their spell time will slow …
O, the Birds of Rhiannon,
forget your head and heartache let go …

Listen to her story –
she can carry you to court
and make you a king.
The Queen of Annwvyn on
her steed of sovereignty,
she has all you need in her bag of plenty.

Anxiety's nurse – she will heal your burden.
As all mothers, she's had to suffer.
Pale muse, dream rider –
her groom was Manawydan.
See her horses come ashore –
she's the Bride of the Ocean.
Hear the Birds of Rhiannon;
under their spell time will slow …
O, the Birds of Rhiannon,
forget your head and heartache let go …

Ride on, ride on, Rhiannon …

Merry Maiden

I dreamt last of Merry Maiden –
she had faery ring fingers and bluebell shoes.
Waking, I still wished I was dreaming
as I asked everywhere what nobody knows.

Have you seen my merry maiden?
She danced all night in
moonfields of dreams.
I long to find my merry maiden –
she sang to me sweet:
'Nothing's what it seems ...'

Meandering down mermaid lanes,
crawling across cromlech moors,
teetering 'tween crack and crag
till my feet and heart were sore.

To the end of the land
I vowed to chase her –
from the first to the last
of old England.

In the hawthorn blossom
did I see her flower hair?
Her golden brow in the shifting sand?

Did I catch her scent
in the pisky wood,
called to the secret cove,
or amongst the thorns and mud
as all day and night I madly roved?

Have you seen my merry maiden?
She danced all night in
moonfields of dreams.
I long to find my merry maiden –
she sang to me sweet:
'Nothing's what it seems …'

Well, the preacher man called her
a tempting demon,
the wise woman a faery leman,
yet, whatever she's called, I yearn to find her –
my many-faced merry maiden.

Was she just a figment of my imagination,
the product of a fevered mind?
Sprite of fancy or soul companion –
she was my Golden Hind.

The rain lashed down when the sun didn't cinder,
I staggered through dark night and cold
but, come Hell or high water, I knew I must woo her
like a knight on a quest of old.

Have you seen my merry maiden?
She danced all night in
moonfields of dreams.
I long to find my merry maiden –
she sang to me sweet:
'Nothing's what it seems …'

Alas, the journey wound on and on,
grey skies did obscure my goal …
yet if we lose sight of our vision
then we risk losing our soul.

I needed shelter from the storm,
till those clouds of unknowing had passed –
a place dry, warm and welcoming …
all I had to do was ask.

I should've known –
home's where the heart is,
my destination was my haven.
Suddenly, it dawned on me –
she was there all along,
my familiar merry maiden.

She took my aching hand,
soothed my weary brow,
saying with a kiss –
it'll all work out somehow.

Together with my merry maiden –
all I ever needed was you.
You're the sweet truth faery,
surely living proof – a fey dream come true!

Merry, merry, merry maiden,
she led me up the path to her garden.
Merry, merry, merry maiden,
she is the stuff that dreams are made on.

Merry, merry, merry maiden …

The Winning of Spring

Adapted from 'Culhwch and Olwen', Mabinogion

This is the ballad of a fatal lady –
the fairest in the land;
her name was Creiddylad,
daughter of Nudd Silverhand.

Her hair was like a river,
her eyes as bright as morn,
O, how she danced in that green, green dress –
elusive as the dawn.

Yet there was a fool who would woo her –
a gentle knight named Gwythyr.
He set out over the mountain
in search of her sweet favour.

He came upon a screaming mound –
it was a burning anthill.
Quickly, he saved it and the occupants said,
'May we one day save you from peril!'

Well, Gwythyr recalled Culhwch –
no less than Arthur's first cousin,
who was trying to win the hand of Olwen,
daughter of the dread giant Yspaddaden.

One of Culhwch's many tasks was to collect
nine thousand grains of linseed …
Gwythyr's little army obliged
and so returned his good deed.

When old Nudd heard of this noble knight
he thought him a suitable suitor.
Creiddylad was not so keen –
but she had little say in the matter.

Yet the day was never to come
that she so haughtily dreaded,
for another was to take her first –
kidnapped at night by Gwynn ap Nudd.

The Dark Lord on his dark horse
swept her back to a glass isle within.
Here he kept her prisoner, declaring,
'You are now my bride – welcome to Ynys Witrin!'

When Gwythyr got wind of this
he was most wondrously wrath.
Gathering his war-band, he declared,
'For his wedding gift I shall give Nudd his death!'

Alas, Gwynn was no mere mortal,
for he dwelled among the dead,
so when they met in battle
it was not his blood that was shed.

Many valiant warriors rode into the fray
and many there did fall;
of Gwythyr's men none escaped but he –
any prisoners were treated cruel.

Among their number were Nwython and his son,
who was known thereafter as Kyledr the Wild.
The father was slain, his heart cut out
and fed to his son beguiled.

Kyledr went wildly mad
and so nearly did Gwythyr with grief –
for he had lost many brothers-in-arms,
as well as his erstwhile wife.

Yet Gwythyr was a goodly man
who did not deserve such calamity,
so when the King heard of his plight
he set forth with a remedy.

Arthur's own knights came to the aid
of him who helped his royal cousin.
The bravest and the best laid seige
to the fortress of Annwvyn.

Nothing could withstand the righteous might
of Pendragon's shining company.
The Dark Lord finally surrendered
and what prisoners were left set free.

Thus Gwynn ap Nudd did not get his bride –
but neither did poor Gwythyr,
for Arthur decreed it wisest
that she returned to her father.

'There shall never be peace here
whilst Creiddylad remain.
Innocent of this slaughter she may be
but she has been the root of much pain.

'Thus, to cease others' suffering
for her heart's consent,
I, Arthur Pendragon,
now do pass this final judgement:

'Every year duel for your beloved
on the first of merry May
until the end of time itself,
when the victor will win his prize

on the very last day.'

Maid Flower Bride

Blodeuwedd, Guinevere, Marion, Niamh,
Blodeuwedd, Guinevere, Marion, Niamh,
Blodeuwedd, Guinevere, Marion, Niamh …

Step within the golden grove
and you may see a maid so green –
in a world of her own devising
where all time and truth is seen.

Naked as the day I saw her,
her spirit as a new sunrise,
glowing, knowing, shining brightly –
a sight so rich for soul sore eyes.

The beatitude of her being
stunned me into still silence –
the magic of her majesty
as I was graced by her presence.

Woodland, lake and moon-glade lady –
hail, fair queen of all Faerie!
Enchantress, muse and woman wisely –
ageless one who is all three.

Unfolding, a face of flowers,
lily nape and snowdrop skin.
Heady bouquet of her bower,
orchid neck, buttercup chin.

Hidden pollen always luring
in her eyes of irises at dawn –
petals perpetually blooming
beneath eyebrows knitted with rose's thorn.

Stamen lashes, catkin lobes,
with lips like split strawberries.
Picking cherry, chewing pith,
and licking tongue of hive honey.

Woodland, lake and moon-glade lady –
hail, fair queen of all Faerie!
Enchantress, muse and woman wisely –
ageless one who is all three.

Peach fur of thigh and forearm,
dusky scent of her passing.
Smooth apples of her bosom
breathlessly ripening.

Cleaving to proud husk of hips,
lunar shyness of her brow,
ivy entwined into locks,
slender sapling, supple bough.

Dancing fronds of her fingers,
tender roots of tendril toes –
whatever they must surely cling to
only her smiling answer knows.

Woodland, lake and moon-glade lady –
hail, fair queen of all Faerie!
Enchantress, muse and woman wisely –
ageless one who is all three.

Under her nectared navel
a warm moss crevice can be gleaned –
a spring inside, a sacred cradle,
from whence all life is weaned.

An endless well, forever thirsty,
whose healing heart is so deep.
Rejuvenating, never empty,
and grave secrets it always keeps.

All I am is thanks to you, ma'am –
wholeheartedly you do possess.
Tempter, lover, mother, teacher,

blessed be, forever Goddess!

One with the Land

I come in many guises,
John Barleycorn and Puck.
Want to find me, pilgrim?
All you have to do is look.

Close your eyes and think of Albion,
spin around and call my name –
y'know, the one who shies from neon
but is of ancient global fame …

Who?

The Green Man –
I grow therefore I am.
The Green Man –
Adam naming Eden.

I've been around since times began
and I may have lent a hand.
Y'see, my forte is creation,
making real what She has planned.

In the caves I became the shaman
with totem, hide and drum –
inspired them with the spark of fire,
fanned their dreams to become human.

With Buddha under the Bodhi Tree
and monkey on a cloud,
to Gilgamesh I was Enkidu –
I died to be wild.

Down in Egypt I was Osiris,
green-skinned consort to the Queen –
torn from serpent to the stars,
there's nowhere I haven't been.

Don't panic when you hear me
going wild with my pipes –
scapegoated as Satan,
but that was mostly sour grapes.

One thing the Romans and Greeks agreed,
I was the god of wine –
Bacchus or Dionysus,
you still see me on pub signs,

Because I'm the Green Man
and foliage frequents my face.
The Green Man,
nature's saving grace.

The Celts called me Cernunnos,
carried me far in their cauldron.
Druids invoked my dragon power
in oaken temples to the sun.

From Taliesin tales to Merlin,
King Arthur to Robin Hood,
and begetting around the Bel-fire
I was the Witches' God.

Alas, the Puritans tried to burn me,
Victorians categorise –
yet no matter how they smother me
my sap will always rise.

With my horn of plenty
I can give you something organic!
Feast on the fruit of planet
without ingredient genetic.

Go on, get your hands dirty;
our Goddess is in peril.
This land's our garden – can you dig it?
It's a matter of survival!

Says I, the Green Man,
ambassador of Earth.
The Green Man
and I'm dying for rebirth.

Who?

Robin Goodfellow

Who is?

Jack-in-the-Green

Who is one?

Green Knight

Who is one with?

Pan

Who is one with the?

Horned God

Who is one with the land?

The Green Man
The Green Men
The Green Women
The Green Children

We are one with the land!
We are one with the land!
We are one with the land!

Heart Wood

The arrow's loosed, the chase is done,
dappled bushes, buds unfold,
the wand is split, the garland won,
unlocking hoard of summer gold.

In the heartwood, how you wooed me,
in the heartwood, neath trysting tree.

Eglantine and apple blossom,
meadowsweet and maytree white,
spring is awakening in the wildwood,
life returning after winter's night.

In the heartwood, how you wooed me,
in the heartwood, neath trysting tree.

With the dew the sap is rising,
scented petals release their spell,
Robin's with Marian in his bower,
honeysuckle and bluebell.

In the heartwood, how you wooed me,
in the heartwood, neath trysting tree.

The leaves are yearning for the sunshine,
the glade echoes with mating call,
for the rain the thirsty roots pine.
Love, the huntress, has us in her thrall.

In the heartwood, how you wooed me,
in the heartwood, neath trysting tree.

When we love the world it gladdens,
leaf and fruit, milk and stream,
Faerie magic is all around us.
May we never wake from this dream.

In the heartwood, Robin and Marian,
in the heartwood, we are one …

In the Name of the Sun

Born from the briefest night, the longest day,
the dream of winter becomes summer light.
Eyes to the east, we wait from dark to bright;
our lord to awake, with drum breath we pray.
Gathered in this free grove of awen's way,
robed, skyclad, blade, stave – all one in his sight.
Hail, noon of the year, the sun at its height,
farthest north, furthest to fall – for pride, pay.

For today our King's enemy appears,
a shadow mars his glorious parade –
oak's usurper, holly sharpens his spears;
after this zenith the splendour shall fade.
Let us revel in his generous gaze,

blessed by the summer sun's bountiful ways.

Praise Song for a Lost Festival

Sun

Oak summer sun – it's Glasters again!
The clans are gathering in the dragon field,
goblin market, canvas city, freak economy –
rainbowgnome-pixiepunk.
Gandalf hats, flamenco frills –
buy the latest festival victim junk.
Veggie burgers and herbal pills
from Babylon Street at Pilton.
Mixing desk, pyramid stage –
you fail to rendezvous,
but you bump into old friends and make some new.
Seasoned veterans making merry,
festival virgins lose their cherry.
Kids take the madness in their stride.
Look! Naked loonies in a mudslide.
Lost sprogs, clogs and dogs,
dropping your torch down the bogs.
Flags rippling, tipis and turbines,
crystal healing and cosmic ley lines.
Watching the world do its thing
within the steel crust-proof ring.
Fellowship of the trip,
surfing the strands of the dreamcatcher maze,
floating the good vibes, the ambient haze.
Banging their drum, nailing their colours to the mast,
timeless mandalas that will not last –
a vision of a dream came true,
finishing the manuscript of Xanadu.

Moon

Fractal cloud sunset,
an oboe and kora duet –
everything is gilded so we don't forget.
Gold leaf patina,
light-spinner, air-juggler,
the city of lights winks on –
the night of earthly delights has begun,
and the punters start shining.
Thank God Glastonbury's back on!
Eavis with flowers, quoting Tennyson.
A topless French girl recites a mermaid poem in German.
Everybody having *that* Glastonbury highlight;
the best band you have ever seen in a marquee
somewhere in the middle of the night.
If only you could remember their name, your name,
where your tent is …
Status: certainly not compos mentis.
Countless connections and misdirections,
chasing the moon lady, looking-glass wizards,
weird visions, glimpses of Avalon.
A million memories flashing and the Faerie city's gone.
Leaving a harvest of tat,
random footwear,
abandoned ransacked tents,
some treasure in the rubbish
mixed in with the human mud,
and just some dazed cows chewing the cud.

Ancestral Mariner

When night and the day are one
he travels the Silver Road –
the moon's shattered mirror –
riding his white-crested stallion.

Rising from the last wave, becloaked
in the dyes of its myriad weave, nets
of bladderwrack tinkling with shells, magic branch
of driftwood helping his sea legs ashore.

Drenched in his father's sweat,
with seaweed mane
and sun-bleached beard
and salty scent of his element.

Grey eyes gleaming fathomlessly
of fabled islands,
sunken kingdoms,
and leviathans.

Manannán, Manawydan,
ogham tongue, ocean son …

Bringing the future from the horizon,
he is the giver of vision.
His ship is thought;
answers are his sword.

Within his sack of crane-skin
he carries the poet's hoard.
At high tide it flows to the brim –
when low its treasures are lacking.

Constant ceaseless, ever fecund,
listen to its flowing song,
lines from the deep tenderly pulling
to where your heart belongs.

Whispering roar
echoing your heart's desire,
soothing heart storms
with the thrumming of his lyre.

Manannán, Manawydan,
ogham tongue, ocean son …

Last Orders for John Barleycorn

Twilighters,
roam with me …

Through the Gates of Herne
to find a kernel of truth,
confront the stag of the seventh tine,
decode the marks of his horned hoof.

Down the familiar paths we trod,
frequenting our earlier selves,
sharing our picnic of the past –
feasting with Pooka and his elves.

Then over the bloodstream
and through the iron turnstiles
          – two into one –
led by the Maiden of the Corn
to the barrow to be reborn.

Along a tunnel to the light –
spurred on sperm, a wheaten worm,
wisely upstream wriggling,
to germinate where we are but a gleam,
prodigal suns returning.

Walking between the worlds,
through fields of alien wheat,
to the place of hallowed dreams
where all our tomorrows meet.

Rising to that yawning cleft –
between that baked earth, right,

and bearded barley, ripe –
beyond all that is left.

Demeter mourns for her lost youth,
russet cloak unleavening
the burgeoning Lammas-scape
in her widowed wake.

Yet, if she lifted up her downcast eyes
they would glimpse a gladdening light
that could demistify those
night-stung tears of dew,

rekindle a faltering love
that was once so bright –
tinderbox heart sparked ablaze
by this Promethean view.

Look! His dazzling smile already melts
her frosty gaze –
the heartening land smiles welcome
as the colour returns to her cheeks.

With a God's eye view
we discerned the canvas
upon which he painted –
pigments selected from a divine palette,
sable-soaked, laden with morning hue –
as elegantly across the vast vista
he swept it.

Drowsy textures arose –
dormant tints, awoken by his touch;
as our orbs imperceptibly peeled
an earthairfirewater colour
was unveiled.

Rich vermilions, sombre umbers,
occult ochres, verdant viridians
were presented by this prismatic parade
as if such a spectrum had never before
dared to emerge from the shade.

Blinded by an unearthly faith,
we now rubbed our eyes
at this dawning creation
with a renewed belief.

Breathtaken, we breathed it back –
pulling the sky towards us
in lungfuls of light – then exhaling,
the clouds dispelled like dandelions.

An impromptu pantheon,
recreating the world
in our image –
raise an eyebrow to influence the air,
lift a finger and the crops would soar,
invert a thumb and harvests fail.

But who are we to judge
when from afar we appear mere
dot-to-dots
yearning for a common thread?

Yet the lionheart's golden mane
is not ours to wantonly flay –
braided bails of spiralling corn
the only evidence
of a God that passed this way.

Now hush, for fields have ears
and silence is as golden as the sun.

From the dancing trees
our forest kith could be heard;
amongst the bustling stalks
the flower kin spread the word.

It was a choral dawn like no other –
the morning eavesdropped upon by Adam
when first he emerged from the All-Mother.

A myriad of voices chattered away,
but in the same tongue spoken.
Revealed! The lost language of the fey –
our ears had awoken!

The gloaming star winked green –
it knew a secret we did not.
The champion waited for
was finally seen, borne in his sacred cot.

Lugh! He soars by bronzed chariot.
Lugh! He strums with a solar lyre.
Lugh! He sings with honey lyric.
Lugh! He sees through eyes of fire.

We toasted the rising king
with wide eyes and barley wine,
our joy expressed in sundancing –
jumping alive with acid mime.

Lost in the landscape of Lughnasadh –
the moment telescoping,
outside time.

It was ourselves looking at our elves
that the Outsiders insighted –

a frame within a frame,
the burning gallery ignited.

Rocketed by déjà vu (again) –
a product of eternal combustion
this glimpse of infinity's spark?
For the answer to that endless question
we had to go where none returns –
down amongst the dead men,
hoping in the dark.

Skull walls leered in silent mockery,
a sarcophagus whistled
a deadly tune –
lulled, rolling into the barrow,
returning to the tomb …

Way, way down there.
A rag, a bone, a hank of hair –
would that be all that is left
to resurrect us?

O Lazarus, O Lazarus.

Ashes to – what then – Ashes?

Dust to – nothing more than – Dust?

As cold clay kissed awake
mannequins of the Fire Drake.

Charged in this earthen kiln,
ossified, lacquered and brittle,
until dropped, and shattered
at the marriage of the Quick and the Dead,
each shard indicative

of the punishment or pleasure
stretching ahead?

No,
not whilst friends remain
to keep one's memory alive –
though tempests torment us,
storms in our cracked cup.
Join hands
and we shall endure.

The dead talked
amongst themselves,
thick as thieves.
They kept their secrets;
we kept our lives.

For now we had descended
to the summit's peak,
casting our reflections
upon the waters of the deep.

It was time to go,
to leave a votive offering behind.
Confronted,
the past's shadow was exchanged
for something of worth to find.

The sacred place resanctified
by rites of passage outworn,
we emerged remembered,
reconciled, reborn.

Crawling into the cotton-budded world,
we learnt to see again, through fields of vision.

Back down to earth
the cloudwalkers gently floated,
the grease of our harvest supper
still upon empty mouths –
terra firmly devoted.

The Bacchanalia was over –
boozy god of derangement
rent asunder: his goodness shared,
blood into wine, flesh into bread.

John Barleycorn is dead!
John Barleycorn is dead!

The parched soil drank him dry:
the Goddess takes back what once was hers.

The power returns to the Mother!
The power returns to the Mother!

As we turn to the crimson-smeared day,
imbibing the drunken sun,
whetstone-slicked sickle in hand,

ready to make hay.

Summer's Wake

The Earth is ablaze with flaming tears,
shed in grief as her sun disappears.

For this is the time of the annual sunset,
when man must savour lest he forget.

A cauldron that tips its molten load –
as it touches the land, Midas glowed.

Reforging the world in a different vein,
making us appreciate whatever will wane.

Leaves become gold to impress their presence –
precious to us in their newfound transience.

Their weight, like their value, seems to have altered –
heavy now they fall, as if indeed moulted.

Gravity and time take their toll,
casting off weight in this seasonal cull.

The reaper scythes with relief –
cutting the chaff from the wheatsheaf.

We reward our labours with indulgence,
seducing our senses with Nature's opulence.

Her dark bounty tempts us to dine,
enticed to sin on the fruits of the vine.

Its bouquet we judge as connoisseur –
our tastes informing us of a good year.

The party is over, the revellers scattered,
the place where it was, in legacy, littered.

A lonely breeze comes to sweep it away;
the rest is absorbed in silent decay.

The garden is a film set deserted,
yet still it is haunted by those departed.

Phantoms flicker of a glory past –
images in sepia fading fast.

We thumb through the album but must let go –
forgetting yesterday, remembering tomorrow.

As the evening arrives our nostrils flare –
a season has passed, scenting night air.

The vessel's absence still ripples makes
as we stand gently rocking in summer's wake.

The dying king sails to the Isle in rest,
where he shall remain the Goddess's guest.

The holly resumes his thorny crown
at his queen's side of blacker gown.

Briefly, the balance is maintained,
as we must gauge what has been gained.

Until the scales begin to sway
and night takes over what once was day.

So rejoice! The year has come of age –
our shadows stretching, like ink down the page.

The Enchantment of Merlin

Like ivy to oak,
clinging, sapping,
Morgan overcame Merlin.

Yet the druid did not resist –
he had wearied of man's folly and pettiness.
His stratagem was implemented;
the pieces of the game were all in place,
wood, water and air.

So, he caved into her
lips and eyes and hair.
By subtle voice and supple caress
he succumbed to the wiles of an enchantress.

Or was that how this legerdemain seemed to us?

What cruel love took place in that grove
only the owl knows,
only the owl knows.

What ancient ritual was enacted
in spellbound Brocéliande
where a magician was enchanted?

She stole the gramarye from the tip
of his tongue,
trapped him with his own cantrips,
perhaps …

As water flowed the words of power.
She bathed in his spring,

drank his magic dry,
leaving him wizened,
with bark skin and creaking limbs –
an old man in wood.

Fool!
She howled
a hollow victory.

Now Morgan held the keys to his mysteries,
but with them came responsibility.
The kingdom was in her
keeping

whilst the warlock was released
from mortal wheel.

He flowed through the roots of the land,
while le Fay was tied to Table Round,
bound by its deceptions and schemes

as awake-walked
our sentinel oak seer,
guiding from afar –
Guardian of Britain,

Merlin's Enclosure
where Arthur dreams …

Wild Hunt

When mad mushrooms bloom
and dream mists still linger,
then restless souls will hear a horn,
the call of Herne the Hunter.

He waits a forest threshold
astride snorting stallion,
garbed in skins,
bow on back,
bright-ringed horn in hand,
a crown of antlers upon his head –
King of the Wood, Herne.

His bestial huntsmen gather
with their phantom pack,
the only sound a chorus of crows
scattered by a second blast.

And the Wild Hunt rides!

Hoof beats shake dew from cobwebs,
leave a whorl of bloody leaves.
They harrow the hollow lanes,
the old straight tracks,
over hedge, through field,
knowing no boundary,
heeding not the law of the landgrabber.

Steed steaming,
breath ragged,
you reach the edge of the grove
where the quarry is cornered.

Dismounting,
spear poised,
you close in for the kill.

Herne waits,
arrow ready,
aiming at you.
He shoots –

then all around the baying of the
Gabriel Hounds
as they tear your soul to shreds.

First,
wormfodder,
earth turning,
earth turning …
Then, reborn –
robin in the berry bush,
otter in the weir,
owl scrying from her bowl,
mouse hushed on wheat ear.
red fox skulking at red dusk,
bristled boar with deadly tusk,
rutting stag of the Royal Tines,
Rex Nemorensis.

Herne
the Hunter
became the hunted.
Animals are we all –
so bless your beast
in time for the feast
and desecrators of the sacred wood
beware!

When winter's tang
sharpens our appetite

and the Wild Hunt rides!

Wolf in the City

There's a wolf loose in the city
he's running through my head
there's a wolf wild within me
and I cannot get to bed

tail swish
dream twitch
muffled bark
bolt awake

wolf opens his eyes
raw amber flashing
yawns as if to swallow the sun
big tongue coiling
arcs his hackled back
claws tenterhook
withdraw

wolf shakes his shaggy mane
of moonlight and brimstone
sniffs the air with salt and pepper snout
and following his nose
he begins to prowl with loping gait

a wolf is loose in the city tonight
all the traffic lights have stuck on amber
cars screech and swerve
to avoid the jaywalker

a red-eyed black beast
snapshot in headlights
a blur of fur against

the glass and steel
pad of leathery paws
on pavement running
through puddles of ink
writing his own lunatic tale
claws scratch on blank stone
searching for a meaning

there's a wolf loose in the city
wanting he knows
not until he finds it
just hunting hunting
with blind instinct
for a scratch for his itch
some heat for his bitch

wolf wants a moon to howl at
some this for his that
chasing tail, the right scent
loitering with intent

there's a wolf loose in the city
slipping into the skin of shadows
flash of silhouette slashing
alleyway, subway, dead-end street

stink marking
his neck of the woods
leaving his signature of animal graffiti
on corners and crossroads
waste ground and no-go zones

There's a wolf loose in the city
he's running through my head
there's a wolf wild within me
and I cannot get to bed

The Wicker Man

Fire in the heart, fire in the head –
our wick is so short,
long live the dead …

Torch my tinder, set me ablaze,
divining sparks skyward rise,
turn my lead into gold,
alchemical treasures untold.

Tribal warmth, selfless light,
dancing the darkness, waking the night.

I am the Wicker Man,
burning up inside,
hollow shell,
nothing to hide.

I am the fuel of my own bonfire,
let my life be my pyre,
not to have lived fully
is the only death.

I want to burn brighter
with my every breath,
leave these wooden bones in a heap;
with wild flames I want to leap.

I am the Wicker Man,
raise my cage to the ground.
Energy is never lost; it goes around.
Losing my skin, the infinite within,
turning on the inside sun,

shining brighter in the shadows
and basking in the glow of the burning now.

The Battle for the Trees

In the besieged glade
the horn-blast fades,

the wood holds its breath.

A stirring of leaves –
thunder of hooves on hollow road,
the horned one rides –
Herne has returned!

Black dogs baying for blood,
wild hunters in the wildwood,
gathering the fallen,
culling those who kill –
outlaw and King's men
in death are equal.

The gauntlet tightens its grip –
overlord versus underdog.
Iron ready, helmets down, jaws set:
determined to destroy.

But thorns scratch, roots clutch,
blind and block
from hew and hack.

When will the axe no longer thirst?
When will the tall trees stop falling?

Oak stands firm,
willow bends,
beech and hornbeam
the strong wind fends –
when it blows
the lesser boughs break,
saplings trampled underfoot,
lives of many seasons topple.

Brief the flowering of warriors,
flows the sap and blood,
written in red the axe ogham,
white corpses in the green.

Black dogs baying for blood,
wild hunters in the wildwood,
gathering the fallen,
culling those who kill –
outlaw and King's men
in death are equal.

Crashing tree, clashing steel,
blade bites wood, splinters bone –
shattered, the peace of the grove.
A deadly toll, this mortal autumn,
many-coloured mantles
stripped from limbs,
bare the arms that claw the air.

The cold wind keens,
skeleton branches creak and whine,
silence comes to the slain,
mouths fill with earth,

eyes gaze beyond,
roots gape through wounds,
rain cleans the battlefield of blood,
enemies embrace the mud.

The Wild Hunt have reaped their harvest,
but before they ride on
their leader turns
to meet his son.

Dark eyes gaze deep;
antlered head nods.

The battle for the trees is won –
but not the war.
The wildwood will live on –
how long for?

All Heal

Between the earth and the stars
it hangs like a threat
of love,
a promise of bliss.
White bubbles to
burst on your lips like a kiss.

This is old druid magic, ancient fertility
rite in your living room,
live in front of plasma screen.
Raise a glass to the golden bough,
to Baldur's bane,
Aeneas' passport to Hades and back.

On oak and lime and apple
how the mistletoe glows
like a swarm of green bees,
berries of awen waiting
for the glint of sickle
in the virgin midwinter sun.

Heather's Spring

There is a spring where hope does flow –
it's nearer than you think,
a place of peace and beauty
where you can go to drink.

Upon a mossy bank
by a weeping bough
sit and spend some time
in the sacred now.

Listen to the gentle song
that the waters sing;
hearken to your heart,
the pulse of its beating.

Immerse and let the music
wash your woes away;
heed the endless melody
that the undines play.

Healing rings around you,
for all your ills a balm.
Waves of love enfold you
in an embrace so warm.

Let the love flow through you,
pouring from every pore,
purifying you with truth,
the beauty that you are.

Thirsty, soul? Come taste
a draught of the infinite.

Baptise this body of water –
let it become light.

Pilgrim, this eternal source
will always replenish.
Blessings of the circle,
return when you so wish.

Remember, all life flows
and will ever renew.
There is a spring where hope does flow
and it is inside you.

The Prophets of Los

Listen to the Prophets of Los …

Magicians of the Imagination,
of eternal voice, of infinite vision,
we chant the dream into reality,
divine omens of other worlds,
pulling the sword from the words,
awaken the Monarch in the many.

Listen to the Prophets of Los …

To the bounty of abandonment,
the freedom of the fearless,
the discoveries of the lost,
finding the healing in painful lessons,
the wisdom of past mistakes,
what lives of brilliant failure!

Listen to the Prophets of Los …

To blow it all in one night
in wild acts of pure art,
to liberate the shining city,
to burn with a stolen fire,
to cry with the wolf,
losing oneself in a deeper wonder.

Listen to the Prophets of Los …

Drinking to the brim,
dancing on the brink,
leaping into the dark,

trembling power, breathless roar,
let the immovable mountain
come to the irresistible shore.

Listen to the Prophets of Los ...

Give me a temple of communion
with a company of the heart.
What new worlds we could create,
what dreams forged out of the manacles of day,
usurping control from the fat conspirators
and with fiery bow storming tomorrow!

Listen, listen!

O invisible brotherhood, sisters of mystery,
bonded by breath and blood,
release the energy of unrealised desires,
of forgotten destinies; resolve into action
the yearnings of our yesterdays,

planting the frail flag of our hopes
on the heights of aspiration,
where another world is possible,
the present not wasted,
the Prophets honoured.

Sunrise Praise

Thank you, Mother Earth,
for holding me in your arms all night
and bringing me back
to a world of light.

Thank you, Father Sun,
for returning to brighten our day.
May you shine for us
and show us the way.

Thank you, Brothers and Sisters,
of water, earth, wood and air.
I shall tread lightly
on this planet we share.

Thank you, Great Mystery.
May we live this day with the wisdom of love,
guided by the blessings of
below and above.

May peace prevail on Earth
and in all our hearts,
love and light to our loved ones
wherever they may be.

So May It Be.

Dragon Dance

All things begin and end
on Albion's ancient Druid rocky shore
William Blake

Out of the dreaming sea
a Rorschach of islands arise.
Born of the brine, cauldron-wise,
cradled by the constant caress of the waves.
Cruel, generous mother,
she jealously guards her brood –
this cluster of rocks thrown together by fate.

Sovereignty of these islands –
Madron, Arianrhod, Danu, Brighid –
by whatever name you're known,
Mother of all, we invoke you.
Brigantia of Britain,
Goddess of the Pretanic Isles,
of Hyperborea,
the Land Beyond the North Wind –
the wind that shapes these shores,
which moves through everything,
the wind of awen, breath of the Muses,
blowing through this pentacle of lands …

From the dawn realm of Logres,
Shakespeare's kingdom of air,
to the suncracked south of Kernow,
realm of fiery sun and foamy sea;

west to green Erin,
realm of the heart and harp;
north to proud Alba,
to the plaid of lowland and highland;
and at their centre the red heart of the Cymru –
Cambria, bright dark land of song.

To this word-hoard of dragon tongue
wanderers added.
All the jewels of the world
have washed up on her shore.

This is Clas Myrddin, Merlin's Enclosure,
made of five proud nations:
independent, distinct, but linked.
Greater than their sum,
a feuding family –
blood stronger than the water
that separates them.

By their pentagram of elements
our circle is cast.
Gods, ancestors, totems and spirits –
grace us with your presence,
with your blessing.

Let the ceremony commence
and the dragons dance!

May the awen descend –
three rays of imbas
filling us
with fire in the head,
wise water below.
Let it flow –
like the sea around these crenellated shores,

entering every inlet, estuary,
cave, arch, gulley and blowhole.

Within and without, awen in all,
coursing through the land.
Earth current serpent lines snaking
– Gaia's tattoos –
meridian points marked by needles of megaliths,
wells and channels of awen,
batteries and store houses of the telluric force
which bless the Five Realms.

Feel it flowing in us all, a genealogy of geology –
DNA double helix, dragon dance of life.

Tectonic tantra, dragon dance,
move with the rhythm, in a trance.
Dance the spiral, circle three,
growing flower, knowing tree.

Dance the dragon,
let the dragon dance me,
biting the tail of infinity.

1 Logres

At white-cliffed dawn
we awake to the east.
In Logres, kingdom of air.
Across the ghostways of the Fens,
Grendel's grave,
North Country fell
to Hadrian's Wall.
What form the Goddess here?
Elegant and fair,

or wild and strong-willed?

Boudicca of the Iceni, come to me!
Defender of these shores,
fierce warrior queen,
fighting the Roman invader.
Air filled with ululating battle cry
that could strike fear into a centurion's tin heart.
Live free or die!

Wide skies, unenclosed fields –
a virgin, fertile prize.
Albion's daughters raped,
invoking revenge and ruin.
England's treasure hoard
fought for by savage men –
Saxon, Viking, Norman, Roman.

As swift as Boudicca's chariot,
piercing as her spear,
east wind streaming blooded hair,
lime-spiked, woad-skinned, savage.

Far seeing Fury – guide my aim,
let my iron strike true.
Sword of the tongue
fighting for you.

Between the earth and the air,
between the fire and the water,
the spirit waits at the centre,
the spirit waits at the centre.

Dance the dragon,
let the dragon dance me,
biting the tail of infinity.

2 Kernow

In the heat of the day,
in the eye of light,
in the land of noon
where the sea is night.

A land of glittering granite,
sun beat-beating down –
a blacksmith's hammer on anvil –
melting us with furnace heat.

The silent longevity of fogou and quoit
marking time. Neolithic sundials –
follow their shadow over moor and shore …
Tintagel to Men-an-Tol,
rag-tree temple, Madron's well.
St Michael's Mount to St Nectan's Glen,
Zennor to Lamorna, this narrow peninsula –

Twrch Trwyth's road,
where legend disappeared beneath the waves,
comb and scissors gleaming between bristles,
like church pew mermaid with comb and mirror.
Ageless Mabon snatching success
from the ears of defeat
before vanishing too … like Arthur … into the mist.

The dying sun journeying beyond, to the sunken land.
Lyonesse of the endless waves, the Fortunate Isles,
of beacon towers, inkdust sand, the semaphore of sails.
Deadly Sillina, adorned with the riches of shipwrecks,
the prayers of fishermen, the tears of fishwives.

Passion fire, soul flame yearning,
in the cauldron love is burning.

The spark on the kindling,
the flint and the tinder,
fire friend, stolen power,
seize the spear of the sun,
long as the day, shadowbright,
give us your light,
give us your light,
give us your light,
so we may do what is right.

Between the earth and the air,
between the fire and the water,
the spirit waits at the centre,
the spirit waits at the centre.

Dance the dragon,
let the dragon dance me,
biting the tail of infinity.

3 Erin

To the wavelapped west now,
to Erin of the green heart –
cleaving peat valleys,
salmon-leaping rivers,
healing holy springs,
roadside shrines of the Lady.
From the Paps of Anu to the Burren,
body of Danu, mother of her people.
Tara, her rounded belly, where kings are born;
Newgrange, tomb of midwinter dawn.
In Kildare the sacred flame of Brighid burns on.
Erin of the Dun Cow, giver of rich cream,
the music flowing like Guinness,
the notes in knots, interweaving,

chasing the craic, a Celtic dreaming.
The dancers' steps move faster,
arms straight, beating down the serpents.

The seannachie's tongue flickers –
like Ogmios chaining ears with his eloquence.

Pilgrimming to bentbacked Croagh Patrick,
the road winds westward,
towards the setting sun,
to the Isles of the Blessed.
The susurration of surf,
amniotic tides, womb of the ocean,
cradling the islands like fragile children.
Into her tender arms
waves of people have rolled ashore –
Firbolg, Fomori, Tuatha Dé Danann …
Conquests and defeats sung by Amergin.

Rain falling in veils of stinging tears,
the watery west calling to our weary hearts,
to the ending of days,
the resting place of ancestors,
where Tír na nÓg beckons us back
to the hall of the fallen,
home of lost heroes,
of Finn, Oisín and Cuchulainn.

Mother Erin, sing me to my rest –
let me rise and fall upon your ocean breast.

Between the earth and the air,
between the fire and the water,
the spirit waits at the centre,
the spirit waits at the centre.

Dance the dragon,
let the dragon dance me,
biting the tail of infinity.

4 Alba

Stern land of stones, of singing bones,
adorning her body like a skull necklace.
Drovers' roads
channelling the snakes of power
around her blue limbs,
crawling up her kundalini spine.

Rock-faced mountain goddess,
recumbent crone, maiden, mother –
moon rolling along your body
like an egg waiting for its time.

By Fingal's Cave beware –
the waters boil in Cailleach's lair.
Over the Bridge of Leaps resides
Scathach of shadowy Skye.

Mother of warriors,
give us strength to defend what we love.

To her we belong –
sons and daughters of the soil.
Our blood we shed to defend it,
to dying breath.
Not for Crown or Parliament,
blue blood or white collar,
the borders and bureaucracy, but
the land itself.

To it we belong –
yet as stewards, not kings.

With claymore, knight me,
pipe and drum, summon me:

From your island stony fastnesses,
from Skara Brae and the Ring of Brodgar,
Callanish to Rannoch Moor,
Loch Lomond to the Eildon Hills,
Harris blackhouse to Stirling Castle.

Goddess of the Gael,
Protectress of the Pict,
we honour you in your high places and your low.

Between the earth and the air,
between the fire and the water,
the spirit waits at the centre,
the spirit waits at the centre.

Dance the dragon,
let the dragon dance me,
biting the tail of infinity.

5 Cambria

Praised land of bards,
realm of the dragon-red heart,
what guise the Lady here?

From Mona's grove-shorn head
to Bardsey's saint-strewn solitude,
the bluestones of Preselau
to ice-crowned Snowdon,

poet's chair of Cader Idris
to king's palace of Caerleon.

With clarsach I call you –

Ceridwen of the Cauldron,
Rhiannon of the Faerie birds,
Arianrhod of the Revolving Caer,
Blodeuwedd, bride of flowers.

Lake maiden, Mari Lwyd,
Goddess of life and death,
from your tarn-dark, bone-white body
a legend was given breath …

Myrddin, Wyrd Merlin, sacrifice, seer,
born of nun and devil, so they whisper.

Below the black-browed mountains,
beneath Vortigern's stronghold,
the boy wizard scried serpents in the midnight cold.
In the tendrils of mist he saw two dragons clash
scaled in the hues of blood and milk,
chthonic heads locked in furious conflict.

Merlin, the ancient child who future saw, said:
White was the Saxon; British the red.
Whilst the dragons fought within
the traitor's tower would not stand.
And while warrior slew warrior
the kingdom would be a wasteland.

As long as they battled there would never be peace –
the dragons as brothers had to embrace.
Together, they would be stronger.
Together, the legacy of Pendragon would linger …

A dream of Camelot, of the Round Table,
a dream of a realm protected by a circle.

Between the earth and the air,
between the fire and the water,
the spirit waits at the centre,
the spirit waits at the centre.

Dance the dragon,
let the dragon dance me,
biting the tail of infinity.

Our circumnavigation is complete.
Returning with wisdom
from the Five Realms –
in our hearts may they meet.

Peace to the spirit of the east.
Peace to the spirit of the south.
Peace to the spirit of the west.
Peace to the spirit of the north.

And peace to the spirit of the centre.

May the circle be open,
yet unbroken –
all hail and farewell,
the awen has spoken.

/|\

The Taliesin Soliloquies

Ceridwen

They call me the Crooked One,
a bent-backed crone –
in the way they mock
all the wise women of the world.
The ones they fear.

Yet I was mother
before I became hag.
Suckled two children from my dugs,
a daughter and a son –
as different as day and night.
One fair as the spring sun,
the other foul as winter's midnight.
I loved them both, of course,
as only a mother can.
I wanted the best for them
and what fortune did not provide
I would with my cunning art.
I gathered the ingredients
to brew a potion of inspiration
from barley, acorns, honey, bull's blood and ivy,
from the five trees of power,
to give to my son inspiration,
imbue him with imbas.

His Utter Darkness I shall spark
with the shining brow.

With my cariad I shall give him cerddeu.
I shall brew for him with my love
the awen of the world.

Tegid Foel

Who remembers me?
The absent father in your memory.
Before I became a cameo
in that whippersnapper's tale
I was Chief of Penllyn,
five parishes to my name.
A city it is said
and a secret bride
by a magic well –
a fairy tale romance –
until one day the fool forgot
the daily task
to cover the well – Ffynon Gawr.
Some say it was an itinerant minstrel
distracted by a bird (so he says).
Lured to a hillside of dreams,
he awoke to behold
what his negligence had caused –
a lake where once there was none,
his harp afloat upon its surface.
At least they named it after me –
Llyn Tegid – it has a nice ring to it,

doesn't it?
And some say I still dwell
below its surface
with my mysterious bride
in my lost city.
And we have not been neglectful in our duties –
the waters are the playground of
Plant Annwn, the Children of the Deep.
It's whispered I may be even the father of
Y Twlwyth Teg themselves!
Fairy godfather, perhaps.

How I had time to sire so many
on that old witch,
Lord knows!

Loins of the father,
cool in Bala's green depths,
let its monsters in fathomless mystery keep.

Creirwy

Fair-face I was named –
a harsh prophecy to live up to.
Who looks below the surface
of my beauty?
Ungrateful, some might mutter,
considering my less-blessed brother –
but who spares a moment,
an iota of compassion,
for Creirwy?
Forever typecast
to be the beautiful one –
a maiden whose role
it is to be fair,
and nothing more.
No brains, no soul
in here, oh no.
I'm a mirror to your desire,
doomed to be its object.
Yet what of my yearnings?
Do I not look out?
Gaze if you must,
yet let me be more
than just the receptacle of your lust.

Let me have my own story.

Beauty is a quality of the soul.
I am the pure seed in all;
I simply need water, sun and soil
to bloom to my potential.
Allowed to grow, I will.
Not kept, contained,
within this dress of thorns.

Afaggdu

Shadow is my skin;
I am night-in-the-day,
Dusk-lurker,
Gloom-hair.
I bear my own pall –
my footprints
a puddle of inky peat.
Black-plumed,
bedraggled,
Ceridwen's sea-crow,
first-born forgotten son.

I know not the light of awen,
no shining brow for me.
Forever the darkness
of my own ignorance.

Denied a sip from the cauldron
thrice-brewed for me,
I would savour its aroma of magic,
watch from the dark
as the village lad stirred,
the old man stoked.
All this effort, just for me.
I knew my mother's love,
if no one else's.
The cauldron split, its hot broth spilt,
my awen wasted, in a flash.
I returned to the lightless place
the negative space of my life.
Taliesin's bane, curdled with envy –
my eyes green in the edges of the world
waiting.

Gwion Bach

I did not know it was destiny
when the old witch came a-knocking,
asking for help.
Gainful employment, she said –
a year's graft,
for a bed, grub, a shirt on your back.
I was just one extra mouth to feed
in a house with too many sticky siblings
vying for the best crust.
To be honest, I was glad to leave.
It was my smeuse out of there,
from a family in which I felt I never belonged.
The others teased me – said the witch would
gobble me up. I was for her pot,
not its stirrer. Of course,
they were greener than witch's hair.
Off I went to her lair,
without so much as a backward glance
at my poor Ma. Her little Gwion
would never see her again.
As Taliesin I would return to Llanfair.
Would she recognise me, shining-browed
Bard of Kings with the gift of tongues?
For now, I had to eat humble pie,
or at least stir it.
Watching the spoon
go round and round. The heady fumes of
the witch's brew making me drowsy …
a moment's lapse,
a sudden splash,
and my world would change.

Morda

There is a knack to lighting a good fire,
the hearth, a cradle for new life.
Strike the flint on to tinder's fuzz,
catch the spark, the fiery seed,
coax it into being,
blow gentle – lover, dandelion.
There's satisfaction to watching the smoke
snake out of your fingers,
the saplings of flame shoot up.
Nest it in its fire house –
apply the tiniest of kindling,
growing in size
like a baby's bones.
Nursing it to independence,
a wet nurse of fire.
Shower it with attention,
the countless kindnesses
by which we keep love sweet.
Keep your heart-fire happy
and she'll keep you merry and warm at night.
Neglect her, take her for granted
and she'll freeze you out.
Given her head, she'll soon get that pot simmering
as round as pregnancy,
that blackened iron cauldron of awen.
They've got a village lad to stir it,
Wipe-nose, good-for-nothing.
I do my best to teach him some sense
in the time we have.
Talk about wet behind the ears!
Greenwing,
he would've dropped the spoon by now

if not for me. If you're going to do a job,
do it properly, I'd tell him. Watch and learn, boy.
Perhaps something rubbed off. I warmed to the lad –
he hadn't known his dad. Hadn't been taught,
given attention. Suddenly left
with responsibility.
Don't let it go to your head, I said.
Next thing I know, the cauldron cracked –
Gwion bloody Bach fled.
Blinded by smoke and steam
as the contents poured into Gwyddno's stream.
By the time I wiped the tears away,
the Crooked One came,
spitting feathers, snatching a brand,
and poked my eye out.

Hare

Crazy-eyed,
I high-tail it
away from Ceridwen's lair,
jink-jinking to
avoid my pursuer
snapping at my heels –
relentless as death,
inescapable as my shadow.
Heart beating its tattoo of flight,
legs thrum, a drummer boy's sticks.
Through cwm, over bryn, cefn, coed,
the gaps between the awkward spaces,
through a hedge backwards, this-way-that –
a mad man's mind.
Method to my erratic path,
yet always her hot breath at my back.
Driven by the fire in my
streamlined head, an arrow of fur,
long ears swept back,
best paws forward. Rabbit foot, bring me luck.
Ablaze with awen,
the world transformed
into a landscape of scent and sound,
predator and prey. Forage, territory and fate.
Moon-boxer,
I must turn and face my foe –
run through the fire
and be transformed.
Let the fith-fath change me.

That which is fixed dies.

Greyhound

I'll teach that young upstart.
This new dog's got old tricks –
the fith-fath he fled with.
Long dog now am I,
deadly Sirius,
death at his heels,
snapping, slavering –
a knife thrust, forever forward,
fangs bared in tight death grin,
eyes on fire,
I shall never blink,
never lose sight of my prey.
As swift as a wish-hound
running through the sky,
the night, my road,
harrowing souls who stray
into the wildwood.
There is nowhere you can hide,
little hare,
no hollow or shadow.
No leverage, leveret.

Your scent leaves a ribbon of bright noise
my nose follows with ease.
I am drawing near,
I taste your fur
on my long tongue.
Little Gwion, you'll make a toothsome morsel,
replace the potion you have stolen,
the awen usurped
from my son.

Hare-thief, there's no taboo
that will stop me eating you,
the darkness to devour you
in one gigantic
gulp.

Salmon

Scales glittering like water in the sun –
a fast-running river
sweeping away all stagnant energy.
I am long-memory,
the oldest of animals,
though newly born
by my stolen art.
I slipped free of death's jaws,
shed fur; my moonwarm blood,
came to the waters for rebirth.
Sliding through a glassy world,
hidden to the human eye.
Escaping by the skin of my teeth,
drawn by instinct
back to the source –
by urgent need
to seed the soil that sired me.
Leap the waterfalls,
run the gauntlet of rapids,
predators,
ever pushing forward –
one slip and I'll be swept back.
A river of questions searching
for their ocean answer.
To push or surrender to the flow,
yield to her deciduous embrace?

Otter

I am water-dog, wave-dancer,
the river my playground.
Sleek-head, ripple-eye,
the wet flames of my fur,
the dripping snout of my muzzle
hiding a grin of fangs.
I am the comedian of death,
fate's fool.
I shall hunt you down,
be your shadow,
never ceasing.
When the time is right,
I shall pounce, seize you in my jaws
and you'll not stand a chance.
You'll be mine –
hook, line and sinker.
And yet,
I am a child of joy,
I know the secret of play.
I'll dry your feet, saint or no,
and await your blessing.
I'll cover your harp;
I'll keep you from harm.
Fill me with red gold, Hreidmar's eldest,
the blood-price of the magician's son.
Watch me dance in the brightening current
and you'll forget your woes.
Yet once my teeth are in you,
there is no escape.
Cold-hearted kelpie,
I will drown you in my element.
My river shall be your grave.

Wren

All the birds of the forest
gave me their plumage
except flower-face,
cursed of the sun.
I am the smallest
but I fly the highest.
Through my cunning
I become king.
Yet that crown places
a prized price on my head.
Sunbird,
they hunt me at midwinter –
those wren boys.
Sticky fingers reach
into my round nest
wren house.
King for a day,
then cruelly slain,
as I must die
so the true king
within me
can live.
Cave-dweller, eavesdropper,
doomed to dwell in a gilded cage.
Counting the numbered days
until my destiny's sharp edge.
I must perish for my people.
The smallest must
become smaller.
With gramarye from cauldron wrung,
wrench my quintessence
from the vengeful air.

Hawk

I will catch you with my eyes alone,
freeze you in mid-flight.
Fierce-stare,
my shriek splits the sky.
Wind-hover,
I am master of the air.
I am the calm at the centre of the storm,
the eye of the tempest.
Nothing escapes my lightning gaze.
You cannot hide, little bird.
The slightest movement and I shall strike.
My fatal blow, the last thing you'll know.
My talons, the reaper's sickle.
My beak will break your neck.
Why fear? You won't feel a thing
when you're dead.

I have a whole autumn
in my feathers.
Sharp-shadow,
I wear the forest's shroud.
I am the birthmark on the sun's face.
I come to blot out your light,
the last thing you'll ever see.

Death's friend,
let me free you
from your tiny parcel of soul.

Grain of Wheat

Listen
amongst glistening ears of wheat,
hear my tiny heartbeat,
a mouse's feet.
Hiding on this threshing floor
from Ceridwen's impeccable wrath.
I have been hot-blooded and cold,
scale and feather and fur –
many skins have I shed
to escape the crooked one's fury.
Will the chase never end?

Stillness now is my best friend.

Hide in plain sight,
one of the crowd.
A poet's fate I would fight.
Give me mundanity,
run-of-the-mill respite.
Yet, I am Henwen's tears.
With my body bread can bake,
beer can brew.

Transformations never end,
only you.

Soul-winnow on life's threshing floor,
strip away the husks
until only the quintessence remains,
the divine spark, let out the light,
with the Uncreated One,
reunite. Relief in release

from this body, this burden
of being individual,
separate from the source.

Why struggle any longer?

At this ultimate threshold
I shall yield.
This field of potential will be my fire.

Come, dark crone,
pluck me from the dust –
take the bones of my being,
crush me to ash-flour
in the mill of time.

Black Hen

There is no hiding from me.

I am the destroyer of worlds. I am Carrion's Queen,
Valkyrie, Kali, Cailleach, the Morrigan,
the Washer at the Ford.

I will strip away all that is non-essential.
I will find your weakest point
and tear you apart.

And yet,
I only have your best intentions at heart,
I want you to show your truth.

I will only snatch you
if you stray from your path,
if you lose your centre,
if you lie to yourself.

I am the black mirror –
your soul's dark night.
The blind maw, your worst fear,
the smothering mother
who on her young feeds.
Never fulfilled,
a raw hole of need.

Black Annis, Baba Yaga,
there's no escaping my hunger.
Let me eat you, obliterate you,
taste your strength.

If you are strong, you will endure.

Denial is another dying.
Death only takes from you
what you refuse to give.
Release into
the serenity
of oblivion.

Twice-Born

The sea is my cradle, my mother.
I rise and fall to her swell and swirl,
her briny breath.

From the crack in my leather bag,
sodden with salt spray,
I see the exclamation of sky and wave –
blue, white, turquoise,
I hear the keen of gulls.
One landed on my tiny craft,

my planet coracle,

and pecked at my caul
Ceridwen had placed about me –
her single act of kindness,
slipping out past her cruel demeanour.
It broke her to let me go,
but I know she had to –

Afaggdu's eyes, daggers
he would plunge into me
given half the chance.

And I forgive her. It was
an act of goddess,
and now I dance in the chaos –
beyond the ninth wave, the tenth,
in the lap of the gods.
Through night's belly,

my brow, my beacon,

a frail light in the vastness,
a candle in the storm.

And yet,
even the darkest night shall pass.

Ragged flags of hope will flutter in the dawn
as we rub rough dreams from our eyes.

I have been Gwion,
I tasted the cauldron

and now I am Twice-Born.

Elphin

Hapless fool am I,
good-for-nothing no good boyo.

So my father says.

I cannot even catch a fish
in his salmon weir –
sticking out into the ocean,
a licked finger in the wind.
Hoping for a change in fortune,
a winning tide,
to take our run of bad luck away.

Here am I
on Beltane Eve
when a young man like me
should be making merry in the greenwood
with a bonny maid –
gathering blooms; washing head in mossy dew.

Instead, my wyrd is to sit,
wait for something to bite.

What do I want from life?
What riches do I wish to be mine?
If fishes were wishes,
which would I catch?
Fame? Fortune? Power?
(Like Uncle Maelgwyn)

A warm bed and a hot woman would do me now.

I cannot stomach
the prospect of returning to my father
empty-handed.
It would just confirm his opinion of me,

a failure.

What will I amount to?
What is my destiny?
Is my story out there, in that wild chaos,
waiting to be caught,
to be hauled in, landed, gutted, cooked?

If only more than my thoughts
snagged on the basket-rack
of Sarn Cynfelyn.

Gwyddno

I am always waiting,
the anxious father –
poised like my namesake,
Craneshanks,
casting my thin shadow
on the waters of the deep.

Watching,
watching for that useless son
to return from the weir.
Even when fortune lands in his lap,
through his fingers he lets it slip.
A wealth of salmon awaits him,
a hundred pounds in his nets –
probably. O prodigal mine,
when will you bloody return?

My crane bag is full of
the sea's vast treasures.
Cantre'r Gwaelod is my kingdom,
the Lowest Hundred –
sixteen cities under my name –
and now under the sea
thanks to that drunken dotard Seithenyn.
Curse the one who failed in his duties –
unsluiced, the waves rolled in
like a stampede of ghost-horses
and covered my plain
where I had stood, perpendicular,
on my spindly heron legs.

And now they mock me
with thrones of feather and wax.
Who can withstand the tides of fate?

The southerning birds
write their druid secrets in the sky
and my soul flies with them.

The sovereign of the sun
slips into the purse of night,
but I am ill-fortuned upon this cruel coast.

Arianrhod, turn your caer
towards me.

Maelgwyn

Some call me cruel,
but try and wear a crown
and see how easy it is to control.

One must mete mercy with severity,
otherwise no one knows the boundaries
and things fall apart.

Someone has to be in charge.

From the hard rocks of Deganwy
I rule the wild fastness of Wales.
In uncertain times
people like a strong leader.

To rule wolves you have to be
fiercer, mightier, wilier
than the rest.

What is the point in having fangs
if you don't bare them occasionally?

What is a growl without a bite?

And yet I am not uncultured.
Let it not be said I am a brute, a savage thug;
my court hosts famous feasts.
Four and twenty bards eat at my table.
Poetry, harp, song
fill the hall every night.
Am I not, then, patron of the arts?
Do not the three strains win over the hearts,
their minds – and then they are mine.
Distracted from the ugly mundanity
by the minstrel's glamour.
Keep the people happy with their tales and festivals
and they'll endure the harshest yoke.
Impress the guests with sly generosity,
cozen the nobility, give them
the illusion of liberty.
Keep your friends close,
your enemies closer,
and you'll rule the fools
with a velvet fist.

Eurgain

I am Maelgwyn's real treasure –
Brightgold he named me,
the fairest thing in his life.
Even in the darkest hearts
a gleam may glimmer
of all they are not.
Any kindness or grace that my father
may possess
he stored in me, his treasure chest –
kept his heart in a strong box –
and gave me the key.
The mead horn I bore
in my father's hall –
summer's tears,
the golden liquid
did not run dry.

A young maiden no more,
now that Elidyr has wifed me,
we have made our home
on the fort of the bear –
round-backed hill,
it presents its broad shadow
to the biting sea
and licks its paws of honey,

deep in its own wintering.

The yellow plague will take my father,

Now that he is bereft of his
bright-gold darling.

The sun had left his life, he said,
when I departed my father's fort.
And what can follow?

Only night.

Rhun and the Ring

I am the henchman who makes
all tyranny possible.
Without me to do their dirty work,
how would they rule the world?

There's always somebody willing
to do worse for less.

They sent me to test
the virtue of Elphin's wife.
He had boasted she was beyond compare –
a moral paragon who outshone
the women of Maelgwyn's court.
Rash words that landed him in the dungeon,
nephew or no.

Silver chains, they say,
but no blue blood will save him
if his boast proves idle.
I take pride in my work.
I'm a professional.
With Maelgwyn's horses and Maelgwyn's men
I made my way to Gwyddno's hall.

There I met Elphin's wife.
She was easy to seduce.
When drunk asleep
I cut off her wedding finger,
ring and all,
and took it back
to Maelgwyn's court –
evidence of Elphin's wife's fickle heart, I claimed.

Alas, Elphin, brought out of his cell,
refuted this, pointing out
the flour beneath the nail,
the untrimmed horn.
His wife never baked bread,
never forgot to trim her cuticles.

O faithless woman, I am deceived!

That young whelp with the strange eyes,
the shining brow,
he knew I was coming, the colour of my trade.
A maidservant they must have used,
and I misused,
and now I face Maelgwyn's wrath.

Taliesin

I hail from the realm of the summer stars –
I am the living memory of Merlin.
My lord, Elphin, caught me in a weir.
His bard I became: behold, Taliesin.

Yet this is but one branch of my ancestry,
before I was a boy as old as history …

I have been
a mountain hare, crazy-eyed, tail high,
I have been
a silver salmon swimming upstream,
I have been
the king of the birds, catching sky,
I have been
a wheaten seed of golden gleam –
swallowed into the belly of the Black Hen,
by White Sow reborn,
a helpless babe on a boundless sea –
deep waters where I was also the wind's shadow,
the wrathful wave upon promontory.

My eyes are the fiery tears of the sun,
my muse from the Moon Queen's Cauldron.
Poetry is my spear;
I am a warrior of words!
I know the lays of this land
and the language of birds,
the tongue of stone,
the song of trees
and the forest of your families.

I know the first name of constellations,
the blessed ancestors
and the Undying Ones.

I was born when the world was still in womb;
I shall be with humanity till the crack of doom.
Proud kingdoms I have seen ebb and flow;
their glory I have sung and echoed their woe.

My curriculum vitae is universal and timeless;
I am the quicksilver serpent of the caduceus.
By fire and fur and feather and scale,

I, Taliesin, bid thee hail!

Prayer for Awen

Let the awen descend, star-crowned, immortal,
from the citadel of the silver wheel,
from the dark secrets of the sky.

Through the torn edges of night she slips –
between the blink of an eye, a waking dream.
She comes unbidden, by her own volition,
inviolate, invading my mind,
bringing her rich dowry of words,
wearing her dress of sound.

Three rays of light
trepanning my mind
bringing me inspiration.

She walks into my head –
pale, tall and dark,
or a fiery spring maiden.
In the crackle between fingertips and
keyboard, page and pen –
æther made manifest, elusive, mysterious.

Three rays of light
trepanning my mind
bringing me eloquence.

O fickle, loyal, muse,
grant me your grace –
generous, callous,
cruel and gentle,
otherworldly, wild
and elemental.

Three rays of light
trepanning my mind
bringing me wisdom.

O Goddess descend,
guide my hand.
May I channel your beautiful truth –
a stream-bed of clear mountain water.
Let the awen pour through me
as tears of tender ecstasy.

Thirteen Treasures

Born of the People's Strength

Landlocked,

he sleeps upon a bed of Jurassic rock,
his slumbering gravity
pulling the ruckled sheets of the land
towards him –
England's mattress
sinking beneath his obstinate centre.

So long has he slept
that even the local flea circus
have forgotten whose skin
they inhabit.

Although he chose a grassleaf mattress
with the Shire's softer hill
for his pillow,
his blanket is now concrete,
smothered by cement,
bedbound with bedsore
industrial developments,
scabby housing schemes,
his limbs scarred roads,
his sweat toxic, breath corrupt.

Yet still the giant dreams –
visions rising, strange as gas,
asphyxiating some with apathy …

intoxicating others
with the music of the swamp.

In bedsits and wine bars
the seers and idiot savants
decode his thoughts,
interpreting the sound his body makes,
the blind movements of his eyes –
examining Morphean emanations
for a clue to his identity.

When his name is remembered he will awaken.

He has slept for centuries,
sand grains softening blasted features –
though one can glimpse his eroded profile
(just look sidhe-ways and you will see)

market-place belly,
tunnel intestines,
jetty fingers,
lighthouse cock,
cinema eyes,
bus-station backside,
precinct ribs,
factory bowels,
shoe-leather toes,
canal-bridge knees,
hill-fort hair,

and abbey heart.

The Old Man of Hamtun
endures still,
his heartbeat heard in every citizen's step
despite the ills he has endured –

his castle crown crushed,
his Catholic robes burnt,
his glorious hands broken,
his arcade spine splintered,
his cobble skull cracked.

And yet,
he will not die,
for his soul still lingers,
his banked fire embers

in every hometown child.

Northampton

The Green Abbey

By salmon wisdom I am ever returning
along that avenue of gothic oaks,
towards the white clock tower, still,
above the bolted coach house.

Perambulating about
this accumulation of architecture:
the sandstone hourglass
of my memory mansion.
The crackle of gravel
my favourite track
of this old record office –
familiar grooves spiralling inward.

Into the dog-eared garden,
past the gravestones of pets –
the ghost of my hound leading me on,
playing with me still in his paradise.
So many times he brought me here,
teaching me to follow my instincts,
to listen to nature,
nurturing my fledgling wild-self –
the boypuppy who became a wolf.

Here in a personal wilderness
I found solace
from the pain of passion,
first and lost loves,
alienation and aloneness.

Discovering solitude
but unable to share its bliss.

In make-believe I found my beloved,
playmates in hide-and-seek with passers-by,
a Jack-in-the-Green, without knowing why.

In this nursery of my imagination
I learnt the alphabet of trees, an Adam
naming them octopus heart monkey.
By a foetid pond with broken maw
I cast a witch in shadowy hut,
and gypsy lights winked
in the gloaming,
grey ladies drifted
in the undead night –
the phantom nuns
who left a legacy of peace
as they paced their sanctuary,
every step a prayer.

And here I repair for their healing grace
when I grow weary of the world –
a taste of the grail
that restores my wasteland
with the memory of summer,
of sun-fat days of timeless youth,
of picnics for virgin palates,
of blind kisses beneath staring stars,
and shadowdancing
under champagne moons.

Where goddesses of fish and cat
enticed from their fastnesses
I gleaned an inkling of the Muse.

And in the grove of my Lord and Lady
I silently communed, vertebrae to bark.
Above, tall and strong,

how they watched me grow –
their heartwood my Axis Mundi,
spine of my history.
Each ring witnessing my full circle –
as past and future pilgrims
rendezvoused with déjà vu
beneath the trysting tree.

Oh, the oaks of my Arcadia,
archive of my life,
endure always –
keep the world at bay.

As in amber be the bowers
of blessed Delapré.

Delapré Abbey, Northampton

Memory Wood

Away from the city's flood
a lost garden can be found.

At Saint Catherine's head,
where the three shires meet,
grows a secret wood.
An enchanted demesne
unbound by human time.

A natural calendar
keeping seasons
amid the ghosts of history.

Wildflowers rise
among the ruins,
the tracks of the past –
the ways less travelled …

Fosseway, Roman,
old coach route,
green lane,
badger labyrinth,
deer maze,
faerie steps.

In the valley of the green rocks
moss sucks up sound.
Listen to the singing
of the Venus of the woods,
the Old Lady's wise silence.

At the pool of poetry
the trickling ripples soothe,
quicksilver mirror reflecting statues.

Above,
the beetling cliffs where castle frowns.
Here tunnel lures
and grotto offers –
guarding mystery,
sacred spring.

Blessed sanctuary,
a place to remember
and forget.

To drink clear water from a well
and to breathe pure air.
To hear oneself think
above the din,
and to bring friends
for this bounty to share.

Rocks East Woodland, meeting point of Somerset, Wiltshire and Gloucestershire

Cooildarry

Cooildarry, a soothing magic
on a sweating day.

Cooildarry, a place of ferns –
moist, green glen of Ellen Vannin.

Cooildarry, a cupped ear of birdsong,
a dawn chorus from the sunrise of Mann.

Cooildarry, eavesdropped upon by
Mesolithic ancestors, curious campers.

Cooildarry, where the waters meet,
estranged by their many windings.

Cooildarry, breathe it in whispers,
and listen to the Celt and Northman
speaking though you.

Cooildarry.

Isle of Man

On Malvern Hills

On these lettered hills I find peace.
Thick as cream the spring
sunshine pours
over the wooded wolds
cloistered from the world.

Here song waits, poised –
a bird at pray; wings worship the air,
waiting
to strike at any fecund second.
The sky is full of poetry,
the green Earth
budding with awen.

From these verdant fonts
Caractacus defended;
Masefield, Browning, Auden
drank. Elgar whistled symphonies
in the silent folds.
Frost and Thomas beheld a moonbow.
Inklings rambled, forging
a landscape of myth and language,
and Langland dreamt his rustic allegory.

From the defiant fastness of Herefordshire
to Worcestershire Beacon,
Malvern town to its tadpole tail –
something positively English
can be gleaned
about this breaching leviathan
of six-hundred-million-year-old granite,
enduring, quietly conquering

all who reach its sanctuary.
From its many wells it suckles all mouths.
Great Mother Malvern.
Her children take
shelter among her skirts,
nourished by selfless springs.

Thank the wild saints,
the spirits of place,
for this hallowed spot,
this bedrock of Albion.

Three Asian lads
on top of British Camp.
I smile. This is theirs too.

Let all hear our kingdom's song:
It is not where you are born;
it is where you belong.

On Ventry Sands

Heading west until the road runs out –
travelling to stillness.
On Ventry Sands
defeating the King of the World.

Time retreats in this Tír na nÓg –
ancient land of the ever young.
Chasing the sunset

to the end of the Old World,
following the moon till morning.

The ocean's susurration
erodes the road's brittle edges.
Here in Dolphin Bay,
where pubs jostle like men at a bar,
we climb singing mountains of the mirror-brine.
Dancing light and shadow
of wave and cloud
that blow both warm and cold –
reflecting the currents of the heart.

Footpaths spiral, grooves in stone,
ruins of cross and sword.
Flotsam of life,
refugees of the western storm,
sheltering on a narrow strand
in ramshackle truck and caravan.

Lost pilgrims gather,
honour friendships
that have made it this far
and, with gaze blessing farewell,
dream the road back home.

Dingle, County Kerry

Prydwen and the Cauldron

Calling you to join the crew – adventure!
Like Bran, Máel Dúin and Brendan, we embark on immrama.
Into the west we steer – beyond the world and under.
Stow your gear, anchors aweigh, we sail with King Arthur!

I, Taliesin, tell you this bold tale,
for I was amongst that noble company
when my liege, the High King, harrowed Annwn
to bring back fabled Cauldron of Plenty.

At dawn three ships cast off from Camelot,
pale sun upon the prow, gleaming on war gear –
and on star-crownèd Arthur, astride the deck of *Prydwen.*
What a ship that was! Shield-flanked, oak-hulled, dragon-sailed.

Poised at stern, I, Pendragon's Penbeirdd,
harped a prayer to Llŷr as we departed –
our destination, ghost-ridden Annwn,
the dark realm of Arawn, Lord of the Dead.

Along the night river of Annwn, winding,
three shipfuls set sail, for cauldron-questing,
seven caers we entered – only seven men returned.

The sea's sad song in ears, spindrift in beards –
for a moon's turning we sailed, to where the sun bled,
till we came to a lonely isle of mist and shade.
Canvas furled, oars manned, into cave we ventured.

Black water sucked, boomed, as into gaping maw
our vessels, like flotsam, were swallowed and swirled.

Frantic flint on tinder, curses, torches lit –
flickering light frail in a deep night world.

The foul air was full of demons shrieking –
maddened crew threw themselves in Brig o' Dread.
Shadow-winged nightmares snatched men screaming.
Our quest, at first threshold, had floundered.

Yet in the abyss Arthur was brightest
and it was by his constant star we steered.
Our oak-hearted king gave us the courage
to fight our foe, to face what we most feared.

Along the night river of Annwn, winding,
three shipfuls set sail, for cauldron-questing,
seven caers we entered – only seven men returned.

Out of the vast night towered Caer Ochren,
bone-cobwebbed castle of the Crooked One,
crone whose cauldron I'd broken: Ceridwen.
'Shining Brow – your awen belongs to my son!'

Suddenly, hot breath of Afagddu: 'Mine!'
Ceridwen's son winnowed our ship like grain.
Yet even the most savage beast, music soothes.
My shadow slumbered: I played the Sleep Strain.

Along the night river of Annwn, winding,
three shipfuls set sail, for cauldron-questing,
seven caers we entered – only seven men returned.

Grim, we moved on, to Caer Fandwy Manddwy,
the wave-walled palace of Manawydan.
Like its protean namesake, it changed shaped,
and many drowned in its fickle motion.

Along the night river of Annwn, winding,
three shipfuls set sail, for cauldron-questing,
seven caers we entered – only seven men returned.

Next, we came to glittering Caer Goludd,
the Royal House of swift-horsed Rhiannon.
All of our unfulfilled dreams mocked us.
Some succumbed to its riches: we raced on.

Along the night river of Annwn, winding,
three shipfuls set sail, for cauldron-questing,
seven caers we entered – only seven men returned.

Ahead, a fortress of skulls, Caer Rigor,
House of Royal Horn, seat of Cernunnos.
Unwary were lured by ivory gates –
but horn called, where only true dreams could pass.

Along the night river of Annwn, winding,
three shipfuls set sail, for cauldron-questing,
seven caers we entered – only seven men returned.

Weary of heart, we came to Caer Feddwyd,
Castle of Carousal, of mighty Bran.
Fallen comrades remembered in mead hall,
songs sung, time slowed and many stayed too long.

Along the night river of Annwn, winding,
three shipfuls set sail, for cauldron-questing,
seven caers we entered – only seven men returned.

Out of the gloaming came Caer Pedyrfan,
four-square seat of the nine sisters of Morgan.
Their treasure – rimmed with pearl, warmed by their breath.
Within we beheld the plentiful cauldron.

Each sailor savoured his favourite food,
some went mad with gluttony or envy –
but it would only serve the Hero's Portion
to those true of heart: we could not linger.

Along the night river of Annwn, winding,
three shipfuls set sail, for cauldron-questing,
seven caers we entered – only seven men returned.

On to the glass citadel of Caer Sidi,
starry seat of ice-crowned Arianrhod.
Through three circles of fire, a fountain sweet,
we drank deep by the Poet's Seat – touchwood.

Spinning, spinning, from Caer Sidi we swept,
till fresh wind keening, with salt tears we wept.

Ragged, we rowed on, to daylight's lintel.
Arawn let us go, on one condition:
Arthur must pledge return when his star fell
and become Annwn's new guardian.

'My agents shall move amongst you;
a final battle will be fought.
To a dark pool you must repair,
and Excalibur by Lady caught.

'Then Morgan's nine will come to fetch your king
in a raven-hulled boat cloaked with shadow.
In it Arthur lay, felled by kith and kin –
for woe's healing to Avalon he must go.'

Along the night river of Annwn, winding,
three shipfuls set sail, for cauldron-questing,
seven caers we entered – only seven men returned.

We had won the prize – at too high a price.
Blinking into the light of a new day,
with the fate-laden cauldron shining bright,
Arthur's ship *Prydwen* wended its wyrd way.

The Red Lady

In 1823 a remarkable discovery took place. Reverend William Buckland, antiquarian Dean of Oxford, excavated a skeleton in the Paviland Cave on the Gower Peninsula, South Wales. The body was buried in red ochre and surrounded by ritual offerings. Buckland thought it was probably a Roman woman. Later examination revealed it to be a young man from 24,000 BCE.

On Gower's limestone horn
where mammoth's bass note shook the tundra
and the bitter-teared feud between the land and sea
gouged a secret gateway between the worlds
a crack in the rock –
beneath golden-lichened cliff –
poets excavate.

Only goats could pick their way there now,
or ardent archaeologists, curious priests.
Buckland was both,
trespassing in the lap of a goddess,
unsteadily treading between the dinosaur egg rocks,
moonscape sodden with seaweed,
umbilicalropeplasticbottleshipsockflipflops
and jetsam of tiny men.

Stumbling into her temple,
sandstone triangle leading to opening,
saltslick walled, giant sheela na gig.
Many she claimed who dared to enter irreverent.

Uncovering something older than his faith's world,
he made it younger. And a different sex.

A crimson Roman prostitute,
or worse, a witch.

Bedded with seashell trinkets, flint teeth, antler tools.
A bone spatula elegant as a letter opener.
Amulet of tusk, ovalsmoothed to sit snug between breasts.
Payment for her favours?

Then what of the mammoth skull misplaced?
What beasts preyed on the loam-silt plain of the Severn
before him they call Christ?
The priest took the Devil in there with him,
discovered a demon, his own.
Branded his revelation the Red Lady of Paviland.

Yet it was a male who lay there
scattered in red. A manchild laid to rest
between his mother and the wall.
Interred from the dawn of time,
only animal memory recalling
Mabon of Wales, primogenitor of his race.
Twenty-six thousand years age his carbon remains.
Older than blue Stonehenge, or the riddled Sphinx,
a Mayan aeon.

Betrothed to this Cave Venus,
he was borne into her red chamber,
taken back up her Palaeolithic birth canal.

Laid in death-cradle
beneath a spirit chimney shaft of light.
Along a waveloud tunnel,
booming with echo of the first ocean,
of amniotic tides, the lullaby breathing of the mother,
offerings left for the man or his keeper?

With psychopomp and ceremony,
equipped for the afterlife.
Stone spears for luck-in-the-hunt,
ochre offering, sacred contract fulfilled.
Undisturbed for millennia so rested
He-who-knows-the-secrets-of-the-earth,
who saw through the skulls of the elders,
danced in the skins of the four-legged,
whittled flutes from the bones of his clan
so he could hear their ghost song.
Until ancestor he became.

A lord sleeping within the earth
before Victorian industry awakened.
Exiled to a more civilised Oxford,
rude Wales lacking a museum to house him,
the red king sleeps amid dreaming spires.

While the real red lady lies neglected.

They missed her completely in their patriarchal myopia –
a mother bereft of child,
broken necklace of shoreline strewn.
Empty-wombed Modron of dragon tribe,
her blood dyeing the land.

The Chair of the Sea

Sitting on the stone chair of Ynys Enlli,
surveying the azure ring of sea
encircling me like a gorsedd robe.

Astride the mountain-hill,
eyes wide,
westering sun shining a bright road
to the Irish horizon.

Mona to the north –
faint, like the ghost of a grove.
Snowdonia's fastness to the west
across the boar's ear of the Llŷn –
Eyri rising, a dream in the distance.
Gwyddno's Bay sweeping south
to the blue stones of Preseli.

Nonchalant sheep and feathered skies
my only witness
as I sing my praises.
Finally awoken by awen,
alive in this sacred moment.

Counting cetaceans like saints.
Twenty thousand, it's told,
sanctify the isle's weathered folds.
Four hundred and forty-four acres
between man and his maker.

Here, where Merlin flies in his sleep
– the veil, thin as vellum –
the Divine glows

through the illuminated runes of ruins,
the vivid hues of the red and white lighthouse,
yellow dory, mustard lichen, seal pup's belly,
brown rams, black-backed cattle, wayward birds.

The book of my dream brought to life.
A road of many words to this point.
The sea's ink waiting for its pen,
the parchment of sky to quench its thirst.

Bardsey Island, Llŷn Peninsula

Thirteen Treasures

Grief-feathered Merlin in his moulting cage,
his mist-lined esplumoir,
watches the world from afar,
its crazy dance, outside time.

From his many-eyed house of glass, he sees;
ageless eyes from seventy windows gaze.
Ganieda's gift, this wise sister's watchtower.

On a lost island found where land ends,
by weary pilgrim's way,
an island in the currents,
by faith or folly's ship reached.

A thin place, no distance between man and God,
where saints cluster, angels on a pinhead,
Arthur's druid dreams, guarding royal hoard.

Dyrnwyn, of Rhydderch the Generous,
white-hilted, flame-edged, true,
fly into hand who asks you,
shunned by all, faithless blade.

Ample Hamper of Gwyddno Garanhir,
long-shanked one's rich basket.
Place food for one man in it,
for a hundred it supplies.

Behold the Horn of Bran the Blessed One –
he of the Singing Head,
time has no meaning with him –
serves the drink that slakes you best.

The Chariot of Morgan the Wealthy,
silver-wheeled and thought-swift,
takes the rider to their desire,
so dream true before boarding.

Finely tooled, the Halter of Clydno Eiddyn,
gleaming with gold fittings,
will lead you to the best horse,
the steed suited for rider.

The keen knife of Llawfrodedd the Horseman,
biting as the North Wind,
as sharp as a fish wife's tongue,
cuts food for four and twenty.

Lo, the Cauldron of Diwrnach the Giant,
fabled cauldron, king's spoil,
warmed by the breath of nine muses,
it will feed the bravest all.

Beware the Whetstone of Tudwal Tudglyd,
stone as cold as death,
heavy as guilt, as blood-price,
any wounding, a mortal blow.

Coat of Padarn Red-Coat, behold the hue,
ruddy fleece of the sunset,
rosehip bush, blush of apples,
of noble birth, wearer show.

The Dish and Crock of Rhygenydd, cleric,
two treasures, tastiest;
steam curls, aromas rise, look:
brimming food beneath the lid.

Living game, the Chessboard of Gwenddolau,
squares of night and bright day;
pawns and queens swapping places,
pieces play themselves: checkmate.

The last treasure, the Mantle of Arthur,
veils the wearer, unseen.
Caswallawn wore it, fell deeds,
Britain's champion reveals.

On threadbare isle of twenty thousand saints
thirteen treasures hidden;
a lost magician guards them,
counting them in wakeful sleep.

Love, the King of Bardsey, Nowhere's Monarch,
Emperor of Nothing.
Island of apples and priests –
deep peace its most precious gift.

House of the Moon

For Thomas and the Muses
(and all guests and residents of the Castle of the Muses)

Hail to the Daughters of Memory,
to the Daughters of the Back of the North Wind –
here in their northern temple,
the Castle of the Muses.
High in the Lowlands,
along a deep and winding lane,
beyond Rest and Be Thankful,
the white noise of the city,
the psychic threshold of Erskine Bridge,
the flanks of Loch Lomond.

A long road north-by-northwest,
into the wild
trusting in Fate –
three to be precise –
the sacred trinity
of Eve's tree.

Before there were nine, there were three.
Before there were three, there was one.

From Belas Knap to Long Meg,
the Three Sisters to Kali's Ness –
following the Serpent Paths of the Goddess.

To the unlikely lanes
of Loch Goil, where
normality runs out.

Here, the castle appears,
caught in a late sunbeam –
the last station of the Celtic twilight.
Angle of incident, the isosceles of
the imagination – where another paradigm intercepts
our own modality. A crack in the door,
too narrow for most to discern.
A druid's portal. The Door of the Derwydd.

You kill the engine
after a long day's ride,
and the effect is euphoric,
a pilgrim's sacred high,
hard won from the road
– the first goddess you must love
to reach here,
invoking Elen of the Ways
to guide you safely to your destination.

To this destiny's nation.

The grandeur of the loch,
the soaring mountainside,
the space and peace
embrace you like a
long-lost relative.
Patiently waiting
for you to arrive.
Prodigal, prodigious, progeny;
journey's son; waydaughter;
you have been travelling here
all of your life.

And when you finally get here
you have all the time in the world.

At the top of a steep gravel lane –
a question mark seeking an answer –
a warm welcome awaits.
Bards and druids, mystics and warriors
await – old/new friends.
Kindled spirits,
a Fellowship of Peace.

Here, you will find what you bring;
discover what you already know;
release, to receive;
give, to let go.
A maze of wisdom,
a hall of broken mirrors,
the Grail lies hidden in plain sight.
Amid the many cups. Take your pick.
The gates of horn and ivory entice,
the doorways to many worlds,
the hearth of the heart.

Home of the Muses. Conceived
in a flash of inspiration –
a bolt of Olympic lightning
released by Zeus in a paroxysm of pleasure –
a nine-night stand with Mnemosyne,
Goddess of Memory.

She doesn't forget.

A blink in the eye of eternity.
A gleam in the eye of God.
The father of a pantheon doesn't fire blanks.
From that union come the three,

then the nine.
The triple-aspect goddess
does the splits –
each daughter three
a fractal conception.
Mandelbrot triplets,
squared.

Hail, Goddesses of Inspiration,
who inspire mankind
to greatness in all the arts
and sciences.
You who warmed the Cauldron of Arthur
with your breath,
deep in the Caer of Annwn.
Daughters of the Wind
– the sacred breath, spiritus,
possessing the poet, the priest, the prophet –
blow upon me,
fill me with your awen.
Lift my quill, and let it fly
across the page in your praise.
Let me worship at your temple,
a mundane shrine to each.

In your mind's eye,
visit the Palace of Memory –
to each room a muse.
Upon whom do you call?
Listen, and then choose …

i

First of all muses
(but don't tell the others I said so)

is Erato – for does not everything come down to love,
the fundamental principle – the God(dess) Particle,
binding Creation together?
What is the manifest universe but the
ultimate act of love.

Let us woo her flowers and words,
with wine and chocolate
dark and seductive.
Priestess of the Sensual –
love in all its forms
and names – from a grope to agape.
The love a craftsman has for his tools;
an artist for his medium;
the marriage of a maker with his muse.
A relationship no one can come between.

Let us call to her
to help us in all matters of the heart –
to navigate the subtle web of relationships,
to see with the eyes of the heart,
to love kindness, gentleness, sensitivity.
As well as wild passion, crazy abandon,
reckless acts of amorous intoxication.
To her we bring heady bouquets of orchids,
a swoon of intoxicating scents and colours.
Let us win her with our sweetest words,
with the lyric sublime, soaring songs.
Let her open our heart like an oyster shell;
give her the pearl of your deepest desire.
She will break you open.
You will fall for her; be a fool for her.

And when she is finished with you
perhaps you shall know wisdom.

ii

Hail to Urania, Goddess-Muse of Astronomy
and all the natural sciences –
here, in this temple of work, of industry.
The office space of the institute.
The captain's chair,
ladder leading to the meditation chamber
and upwards to the stars.
The turret of vision.
But first, let us be down to earth –
let us brew strong coffee
and get down to business!
The hour is late,
and there is much to be done.
The filing and compiling,
refining and finishing,
the connections and communications.

If there were a Muse of the World Wide Web,
the ghost in Tim Berners-Lee's machine,
this would be her –
reaching across the planet
at light speed,
a billion alignments,
synapses firing
across cranial-continents.

Constellations of classical consequence,
let the scientists and astronomers
the far-seers near and far,
be guided by you with humility.
If they glimpse to the heart of Your Mystery,
let them be filled with awe.
Let them see the star inside themselves –

the cosmos inside the man,
and know,

As Above, So Below.

iii

Hail to Calliope,
Goddess of Epic Poetry,
the grand narratives of Homer and Ovid,
the master storytellers of every land –
here, amid the stacks of books and papers
on economics and politics,
shelves sagging with the weight
of history, of great minds,
and deep themes.
No triviality here – whimsy is exiled.
This is a place for profundity,
for thinking big.

And bigger, outside of the box.

Take a reality detox.
It doesn't have to be the way it is.
Other worlds are possible,
with the active ingredient of imagination.
Leaven it with vision.
Let it rise in the oven of love.
Design your new system.
Change the world. Rearrange. Reboot.
Begin again. Take its mad song;
make it better.

But don't forget the past.
Learn from history, from tragedy,

that must never be repeated.
Fight for what is right,
until evil is defeated.
Let the People be the Victor,
not the Dictator.
Let myths be the virus
to bring down the tyrants.

Calliope, grant us your grace.
To complete our own Hero's Journey.
To return with the Elixir
that will Heal the World.

iv

Melpomene, Muse of Tragedy,
we come to greet you,
clad in dark attire,
wearing widows' weeds,
faces covered in ashes,
the mask of sorrow,
weeping for the world.
The vast tragedy of it all.

Yet seeing the beauty
in every small miracle,
the heaven in the disaster zone.

O Melpomene, let us sing your goat-song,
so we do not forget.
So we remember and honour.
Work through our grief,
dance our sorrow
and let go when we're done.
Move on, move on.

Let not our grief become our identity.
It is only a mask, a costume,
for the danse macabre.
The sun still shines; the birds still sing.
The world still turns, saying, Begin! Begin!
Aid us to heal conflict,
to bring peace
through understanding, through empathy.

Time to stop playing soldiers;
time to put down our guns.
Time to dismantle the warheads;
time to defuse the bombs.

Melpomene, from your deep heart
bring peace, end suffering.
You know the depths of humanity's sorrow.
Listen and release it. So.

v

O Polyhymnia – sing your hymns abundant!
To all religions, all faiths, all paths and ways.
Open your heart to all true seekers.
Your songs carry the pilgrims
up all sides of the mountain.
Raise us to higher lands.
Help us to be closer to the Great Creator.
Through prayer and poem,
incantation and chant,
liturgy and mantra.
Through all sacred words
that exalt the praises
of Spirit.

Let us resurrect the Perpetual Choirs.
Strike the tuning fork that will
bring harmony to all
corners of the world.
Let us commune in silence
to hear your song.
Light the candle
and sound the gong.
Speak from the heart
prayers of beautiful truth.

Thanking you for this day
and every day.

Guided by the world's mythologies,
by the saints and sages,
let us create Heaven on Earth –
peace everlasting throughout the ages.
Let all heartfelt prayers be heard
and answered.

Let the Sword of Peace,
the Circled Cross of Truth,
be carried by your Warriors of Love.

vi

O Clio, Muse of History,
of Time's chronicle –
a scroll unscrolling back through the centuries –
let us study your pages,
learn from the past's folly and wisdom,
the triumphs and the tragedies,
of Man – nature's child, run amok,
playing at being King of the World.

Here, in your temple
let us learn the lessons from the chroniclers.
A place of study and reflection.
A lofty mountain summit
from where one can get a perspective.
Eagle-like, the far view –
a gaze that penetrates the wall of time.
Here, the volumes of vision
are catalogued, the undying efforts
of those who carry the Flame of Peace.

A tray of tea things,
a desk of curved wood,
a lamp spotlighting
the scholar's work.
Dictionaries, biographies, encyclopaedias
compass the world's knowledge.

A small red paperback sits, waiting
to be noticed. *Pedagogy of the Oppressed.*

This is a room Che Guevera would have
been comfortable in – sitting with his army boots up,
smoking a large Cuban stogie,
planning his next campaign.
The ongoing liberation
of humanity.

Vive la Revolution!

vii

O Euterpe, Muse of Music,
soothe us with your sweet tunes.
Soften our hearts;

make them soar.
Lighten our souls;
play the Three Chords
of Joy, Sorrow and Sleep.

Paint your colours of sound
in hues of harmony
and discord.
Vibrations of the spectrum,
the wave of the rainbow.
Seduce us with the ear and the eye,
connoisseurs of the world's beauty
and the arts that celebrate it –
sketches, paintings and engravings,
sculptures and frescoes,
prints and photographs.
Let the senses drink in
the deep spirit.

We are beings of colour –
each chakra
a paintwheel of pure pigment
that we dip the brush of the day in.

We are what we shine.

The ultimate works of art,
the ongoing masterpiece
of Creation.
Reality, the canvas
upon which we compose ourselves.

O Muse, guide our hands –
make each day a work of art.

viii

Ah, Thalia – your shrine feels like home.
Muse of the Word – spoken, written, heard.
You wear the comic mask, yet are far more.
Here, you are patroness of all literature,
of the mercurial element of language.
Here, all poetry is praise,
and the play's the thing
to pique a monarch's conscience.

Yet there is lightness too.

Dolls and clowns line your windowsill,
reminding us of the serious business
of living lightly,
with humour, and grace.
Sink into the armchair
and pick your book
from the teetering stacks –
a Glen Coe of collected dreamings –
towering over you.
Don't take one from the bottom
unless you want to start an avalanche!
Buried in words. Where to start?
Trust in serendipity.

Your hand will alight on the right book for the
right time.

This is a library to while away a
winter with.
Steep yourself in ink –
soak in verse, in novels and plays,
and let inspiration well up.
A place to hatch a masterpiece,

to dream up a magnum opus
or the collected works of anonymous.
And discover the true meaning of life,

the simple art of happiness.

ix

O Terpsichore, Muse of the Beautiful Movement,
of the swinging and swaying hips,
the toss of the hair,
the line of an arm and a leg,
graceful and fierce,
balletic bella donna.
Here, your spirit is honoured
with the dance of flames
in a merry hearth.
With the sublimity of candlelight,
the peace flame burning perpetual
and the frivolity of fairy light.

Let your presence be invoked
with many instruments –
with harp and guitar,
didg and djembe,
bodhrán and harmonica.

Let the fingers dance over the strings
and over the keys of night and day.
Here, let the peace pilgrims gather
to share their heartfelt words and songs.

Flags of the worlds
adorn the walls, inviting all nations
to gather in the dance of peace.

Hats of witches and warlocks
are perched on the bannisters,
awaiting the players for the Midnight Masque.

Dirk, hard at work,
cooking up a banquet in the kitchen.
David, on the knight shift,
cutting the logs, gathering kindling,
creating an ambience fit for a goddess.

And every guest offers their blessing.

Tipsily, we wassail you, Terpsichore –
with a hiccup and a stolen kiss.
Let us raise the Farewell Cup
and toast the fellowship, enduring;
the winding road calls us.

May we meet further along the Way.

x

Shining in the centre, the Lord of Light,
Apollo – strum your lyre
high on your rocky crag,
communing with the eagle
on your Scottish Parnassus.
The Muses' lover and conductor,
pupil and instructor.
Around him they dance,
like the Nine Ladies to the Fiddler.
What is a muse without an admirer?
Without someone to inspire?
He is the Rhymer to the Queen of Elfland;
Orpheus to Eurydice; dancing the ancient dance –

his melody holding open the Gates of Death,
staving off oblivion – so something survives of us.
His Art the ultimate Act of Love.

It was said Apollo journeyed north for the winter,
to a temple on the Isles of the Blessed – there to dance
the dark months away to the rhythm of the moon.

Here, in its house,
where peace is forged; and pilgrims
unforget.

Waking the Night

Moon Bathing

Close the language door
and open the love window.
The moon won't use the door,
only the window.
Rumi

Peeling off,
plunging in
to the wet darkness.
Shock of cold,
cries of pain, pleasure.
Feeling alive,
feeling free.
Swimming in you
– a silver road
to your window of love.

After all the words,
there is only the sea,
your skin, the stars,
the benign moon
looking down on you
with love.

A man in blue
calls over from the shore,
telling you this
is not allowed,
that you must come back!

And so you
lie back in the waves,
let your ears fill with brine
and float.
Can they not see
you are clothed in her love
and nothing can touch you?

You do not belong
to their world.

You have broken free.

Lunatic, heretic –
you howl at the moon,
sing the name
of your beloved;
laugh at it all,
the consensus insanity,

the people who take it seriously.

There are always
voices calling from the shore
telling you to come back
to behave. To not break rules.

Why listen?

How can it be
forbidden to
swim in the sea
under the moon,
thinking of your love?

No longer will you heed those voices.

The babble fades, as
you take all the time in the world.

And when you finally emerge,
glistening,
the tourist police await.
You hold out your arms –
'Go on, arrest me!'
– but they walk away,
ashamed
of your nakedness.

They cannot see you are clothed
in her love
and nothing
can touch you
anymore.

Looking Back

I walk towards the light,
wanting to turn around,

wanting the night to fade
with the affirmation of your face,
but I must press ahead
and trust you will make it –
that you will slough your shadow,
the snakes at your heels,
and find your way to the door of day.
I strain to hear your footsteps,
but they are deafened by my heart.
Love bound blind –
my eyes need proof,
but I cannot look.
To doubt, to grow impatient,
and I shall lose you for ever.
I must bide my time
and let your wounds find
their own mending,
your feelings to surface.
Yet how I yearn for
this bitter winter to be our spring.
How slowly rises my bride.
O, to kiss the darkness,
to banish this uncertain silence …

I walk towards the light,
wanting to turn around.

You Are Everywhere I Look

You are everywhere I look:

in my empty bed,
between the pages of a book,
behind my eyelids,
in my waking dream,
on a hypnotic computer screen –
the expectant cursor, your eyelashes,
the shining page, your skin.

I recall the black coffee rush
as you walk into the room.
Remembering fingers caress
the contours of thin air,
your negative space,
the absence of your hair.

I shift my axis to your orbit,
circle your grove,
its bounty in a barren land.

Your music sets me spinning,
strikes the chords of my heart.

A fire thought dead
is rekindled
and on this longest of nights
I turn my gaze
towards your horizon.

Your Love

Your love is a mountain of faith.
It is my pillar to heaven,
my moveable temple.
I take sanctuary in it
and it nourishes me.

Your love gives me the strength
to live my truth.
Armed with your belief
I can accomplish anything.

Your love is my ocean wind,
my guiding star.
It is a proud ship; it is waves breaking.
Your love fills my sails, lifts my flags.

It is the air that feeds my candle flame;
it is the light and it is the darkness,
the night that soothes,
a nest of dreams.

Your love is being
embraced by your eyes,
being seen by your lips,
tasted by your hands.

Your love is a feast,
a dinner prepared with tenderness,
a blessed transformation.

Your love is an act of grace,
a redemption and a release.

It is a prayer and an offering,
a flower that will never wilt.

Your love is a soft rain;
it is a song sung in silence.
I am listening to it now –
the endless syllable between the words.

I float upon it in my sleep.
Waking, I wear it like a cloak,
an invisible cloak
and walk with it protected
                                        an angel at my shoulder
                                                taking me home.

Let Love Be Our River

Let love be our river:
we have far to go –
it will carry us.

It will carry us
on its strong back
in smooth strides.

We do not have to struggle;
merely surrender
to its selfless embrace.

It has travelled far.
It is old and wise.
Within its liquid skeleton

the memory of mountains.
It has known the bitterness of oceans,
the tears of the sky.

Sometimes, it bursts its banks. Overwhelms.
Sometimes its way is blocked by sluices and weirs.
Surrender to ecstasy, the river sings.

The river knows where it is going
even if we cannot see around its bends,
its many strange windings.

It will get us there in the end.
The patient sea
awaits.

Let love be our river;
it will carry us,
it will carry us.

Breaking Light

for J.

i

It is late. It is early.

3 a.m. Too awake to sleep.
Too tired not to.
Feeling the house breathe around me,
its unfamiliar night sounds, a
strange landing.
The pores of my skin
are a million unblinking eyes.
You have set me off
like a spinning top.
Made my head explode with light.

As you lie next to me,
I listen to the white noise
of rain on your attic windows,
whispers in the static.

Even in the city I feel Her near.

Lady Autumn,
I can hear you
washing your long russet hair,
a weeping willow sifting the wind.

The rivulets reveal its lustre,
like a wave-wet pebble on the beach –
your colours unveiled, a whole paintbox.

Everything becomes more beautiful
the more it lets go –
the more it releases its inner life.
The promise of frost brings
the spectrum to the surface –
the colours the light let go of.
We see what isn't absorbed.
A leaf, in Spring, not-green, becomes
in Autumn, not-red.

What the world sees is
what we cannot contain inside us; it
spills out –
breaking light,
the way love splits us open.

ii

It is late. It is early.

Lady Autumn is walking
with sloe-eyed grace
through our lives once again;
rose-hipped, withy-limbed,
bejewelled with blackberries like
tiny bunches of grapes,
ready to burst on your tongue,
lips, fingertips,
stained with juice;
rowan berries, hard as nipples;
elder berries glisten like spider eyes,

from boughs of yellow flames,
watching.

The forest floor
where we made love
sanctified by
your blood, my seed,
mingling with the soil.
Its rich earth of
fertile death
scattered with ash keys, acorns,
fur-flowered beechmast,
horse chestnuts, hard and smooth
in their spiky jackets
(like antiques packed in a sea mine),
the milky bullets of cobs,
walnuts ransacked by Ratatosk
buried in forgotten cists,
fungi erupting from another world,
gills gaping,
like fish gasping for breath.

I graze lazily through your edible forest –
pore my hot breath into your jew's ear,
rifle your king alfred's cakes
and penny buns,
devour your chicken-in-the-woods.

I trace the lace of your mycelia,
the wood's lingerie. I yield
to your moreish morel,
drink champagne from your chanterelle.
You lick my slippery jack,
make my puff balls
explode.

Feral cry in the thicket,
the grunt of wild boar
snuffling out truffles,
the sow's ear of his mate.
A roe deer freezes, wet nostrils twitch,
a flank shivers,
and it leaps into the wood's legend.

The sunlight snags
on the canopy's lattice,
the chlorophyll circuit-board
of a crimson leaf,
the abacus of dew
on a cobweb.

Nature's astonishing
attention to detail
insisting
we notice.

Like an act of love.

I stroke your face
with a tuft of old man's beard,
circumnavigate you with a feather,
all your inlets and promontories.

We cast a limpet shell
on the river
laden with our dreams
and laugh as it sinks.

iii

It is late. It is early.

Lady Autumn
teaches us
the art of letting go,
as she performs her annual yard sale,
de-cluttering with a tut, a smile,
a shake of the head,
tidying away the toys of summer.

She sings as she sweeps –
her long skirts
layered with a patchwork of leaves,
gathering up all that we don't need
in her wake.

Busily she insists
we put our house in order
before the harsher times ahead.
Her winter sister is not so sentimental
when she brings her black bag,
as bottomless as a December night.

Despite all we have done,
the gifts we have squandered,
her treasures plundered,
still the Earth
is beautiful.
Still the Earth will forgive us.
Her compassion is endless,
and we will weep at her feet
before this is played out.

But first, a favourite vinyl crackles

to the centre.
The needle gathers dust.
With a melancholy pang
Lady Autumn revisits her old haunts,
her maiden places,
savouring the memory one last time
before letting it fade.

She presses the best
into the palimpsest of the past,
a bonfire for the rest.
Smoke curlews from the piles of leaves,
gathered into golden dragon hoards,
to be kicked –
and, for a moment,
we are as rich as bank robbers,
the folding gold falling around us.

iv

It is late. It is early.

We finally met
at Lammas –
when summer first seems to sense
its own mortality.
Ours is a late summer love.
Not the foolishness of Spring,
swept along by giddy lusts,
the chancy intoxication of the May,
nor the apparent glory of June,
when midsummer dazzles us
with its gaudy enchantment,

but a love of long shadows,
of languid contentment.

Ripening to prime –
we are ready for love's press.
It insists we offer all.
What can be gained from
withholding the tiniest drop?
Pulp and pith and pip,
let the cloth of truth,
contain our allness.

Gladly we bring our bounty to share
to the harvest supper of the heart.

Arriving in splendour,
wearing our autumn like a crown,
we greet each other
at the end of a long road,
our harlequin robes
stretching behind us.

Stopping to let the sunset slip
like a mug of copper hops
down a thirsty throat
over the blue tapestry of hills
pegged to the sky by trees,
we give thanks for the abundance,
the riches of the year,
strewn before us
with such wild abandon.

Yet the thrift of Mother Earth
means nothing
is wasted.
All the ungathered,

unreachable treasure
that falls on the ground,
unpicked, to rot,
becomes the mulch
from which the future grows.

v

It is late. It is early.

And the world is turning beneath us,
so let us hold onto one another,
for where we go to sleep
is not the same place we wake up.
Everything shifts – the Earth
tilts;
we have only our the axis of our love
to stop us from spinning off into space.

You anchor me
with your eyes,
a touch, a word,
breathed in the night,
a smile at break of day.

We contain each other with such
lightness,
allowing our spaces to dance
against one another.
To make a third shape between.

I inhale you. You exhale me.

I slip into bed, blindly, seeing by heat,
and let the warmth you have left
envelop me.

Our souls fit together,
like our bodies do.

As though,
way back when
before the beginning,
we had been wrought as one,
then, broken apart –
to be finally,
blissfully –
joined once more.

The same light
shining through us both.

Love,
the home where we belong –
the door with our names on –
waiting for us to arrive.

The Secret Commonwealth

A Midsummer Summoning

On Midsummer night, the birds are singing,
the sun sets and the sky draws flame,
In the grove the Bard is strumming,
calling all of Faerie home again.

Come the mist, come moonlight, stars' ancient fire.
Come gather friends, make the flames grow higher.
Spirits bless our circle, peace thrice-wise true.
Let the Way open to worlds of many hue.

The Earth is calm, caught between night and day.
Still the solstice magic lingers in the air.
From dusk's cloak of shadow come the Fey;
the Lordly Ones ride, wild, jewel-eyed and fair.

The Three Sisters

When you are lost on the Way
and the light is failing;
when your legs are weak
and your heart is ailing …

Upon the rise the Sisters await,
Stormhold of your heart
to guide your Fate.

The Maiden is nimble,
her laughter like light.
See her dancing her spells,
learning love's flight.

The Mother is bounty;
she nurses, protects,
giving and guiding.
To her genuflect.

The Crone is the wise one;
her lessons are hard.
She's the Hag of the Mountain,
the Washer at Ford.

O Three Sisters,
we're weaving the loom,
O Three Sisters,
give birth to your doom.

Dancing, Nursing, Destroying…

The Castle of Love

The dancers take their partners
and the game begins.
Whoever loses
is the one who wins.

The rules are changeable
and so very old.
Hearts are optional;
the corridors are cold.

There are secret passages,
mirrors and spies.
The chambers of romance
are cushioned with lies.

Don't look in the cupboards
or under the stairs.
What lurks beneath
will raise a few hairs.

Down in the dungeons
lurk rack and thumbscrew.
In oubliettes of regret
the prisoner is you!

In the Castle of Love,
in the Castle of Love …

[Repeat to fade]

Crows in the Willows

Crows in the willows
toadstools in the grass;
not like our love,
these things will pass …

Be there snow on the furrow
or sun on the dew,
fair weather foul,
I shall follow you.

Should moonlight shatter
on midnight lake
I shall never
you forsake.

Should spring uncoil
and harvests fail,
you shall never
hunger at all.

For I'll always be there for you.
Yes, I shall always care for you.

Crows in the willows,
toadstools in the grass;
not like our love,
these things will pass.

The Morning Song

I broke your heart this morning;
it smashed to the ground.
I keep looking for the pieces
but they can't be found.

Sun, sweet sun, burn the mist away.
Bold bird sing, and welcome the day.

I hid my wounded heart this morning
inside a cuckoo tree.
I went to get it back
and it had become a bee.

Sun, sweet sun, burn the mist away.
Bold bird sing, and welcome the day.

I left my heart on a train this morning
on the shiny luggage rack.
I knew it as the train departed
but I'll never get it back.

Sun, sweet sun, burn the mist away.
Bold bird sing, and welcome the day.

I found my heart this morning,
it was a solid lump of ice –
so I took it to the glasshouse
and followed your advice.

Sun, sweet sun, burn the mist away.
Bold bird sing, and welcome the day.

The world will spin – night becomes dawn.
The seasons turn – a new day is born.

Blood Red Moon

Blood red moon,
the wild is rising.
Blood red moon,
the tide is high.

Blood red moon,
the river's sighing.
Blood red moon,
the trees grow fire.

Can you feel
the sap is stirring?

Can you feel
the lunar bore?

Can you feel
the Earth's quickening?

Can you feel
and feel it more?

Mmm, the Maid is dancing.
Mmm, the Green Man draws near.

Blood red moon,
the wild is rising …

Two Foxes

Two foxes crept through the night,
two foxes, the moon was bright.

One was bold, but had a good heart;
the other was cunning, swift as a dart.

Through shadows they stole,
gaps in the hedge,
down any black hole
and on to the ledge.

Looking for fowl,
looking for trash
binbagsmashandgrab,
time to dash.

Out goes one,
the other comes in,
kindness, badness,
thick and thin.

As different as night and day,
two foxes, out to play.
Which one's right?
Which one's wrong?

Answer that,
and it's a different song …

Schiehallion

Schiehallion is calling to me,
Schiehallion, palace of the Sidhe.
Schiehallion is where I want to be,
Schiehallion, mountain of Faerie.

Climbing to the sky,
each step a prayer –
a silent ascent
walking on air.

The way is winding,
our fate unclear.
Trust in the path;
put aside your fear.

When you reach the peak,
all is still.
Look at what you can achieve
with your will.

You must surrender
to truly gain;
leave behind your armour,
let out your pain.

The mountain is strong,
ancient and wise.
Let it hold you up,
and open your eyes.

Behold the beauty
that is at your feet.

The wonder of the world
that you complete.

Old Friend

Old friend, old friend,
don't you know, don't you know …

The road you set out on full of hope
will be full of snags and twists.
All those shiny dreams of tomorrow
will make you a pessimist.

Old friend, old friend,
don't you know, don't you know …

From the moment you come out wailing
you've been dying all these years.
Sometimes the only way to keep on living
is to drive on through the tears.

Old friend, old friend,
don't you know, don't you know …

Each farewell breaks my heart,
a sunset with no encore.
So savour each moment, hell!
That's what being alive is for.

Old friend, old friend,
don't you know, don't you know …

Many fall by the wayside
but true friends stay with you.
Tumbleweed heart, turn the wheel,
trust to the wind and roll on through …

Follow the Sun Road Home

Waking to a dreaming world,
the road winding,
ancient shadows in the land,
the mist rising …

The brook running deep and clear
to the slumbering barrow on the hill.
Crossing the faerie bridge with a kiss,
the door to the Otherworld is there still.

Follow the sun road home
called by the song of the Sidhe.
Follow the sun road home
over the Westering Sea
beyond this world of bones
to the place where the spirit is free.

Within the chambered tomb
we wait for the crack of dawn.
Within the dripping darkness
we wait to be reborn.

In the stillness and the silence
we listen to our forefathers;
before the horn of solstice blows
heed the heartbeat of the Mother.

Follow the sun road home
called by the song of the Sidhe.
Follow the sun road home
over the Westering Sea

beyond this world of bones
to the place where the spirit is free.

The gathered hold their breath,
feel the thrill of Earth's quickening –
gaze through the grey and pray,
a grail for the sickening.

A swift kestrel takes wing,
the sun has risen, has risen –
friends depart and wheels turn.
May we meet over the horizon.

Follow the sun road home
called by the song of the Sidhe.
Follow the sun road home
over the Westering Sea
beyond this world of bones
to the place where the spirit is free.

Down hollow lanes and shining leys
follow the sun road home.
Down hollow lanes and shining leys
follow the sun road home …

Those Who Have Gone

Can you hear them in the sage brush?
hear them in the rain?
Whispers in the canyon,
thunder on the plain.

Footprints on the desert floor,
red hand in cave shadow.
Beasts seen from high above,
lines too long to follow.

They linger in the place names,
in old customs, in a word.
They speak to us in dreams,
in songs that cannot be heard.

They are the first people,
those who have gone.

They are the wise children,
those who have gone.

They are the silent stewards,
those who have gone.

They live on in us,
those who have gone.

The Love of the Land

Dragons of War

Kernow and Cambria, Erin and Alba –
Logres, alas, Logres …

Red skies, black seas,
yellow rivers, naked trees.
The Earth she is keening –
can you hear her, can you hear?

The days they darken,
a bitter rain falls,
the people are weeping
while the Mad Kings rule.

Above, beating thunder –
our doom draws near.
Look up in wonder;
fall to knees in fear.

Fang and wing,
flame and claw –
the dragons of Albion
make war, make war.

The land it is wounded;
the kingdom it bleeds.
It is a gun age, a bomb age;
the carrion birds feed.

Where are the heroes?
Where is our King?
In the time of the Reckoning
only the bravest shall win.

Windsmith against whirlwind,
agents of harmony, discord,
armies clash at dawn and dusk –
words of power versus
the silence of swords.

The dearest are taken.
What is the cost?
Is this worth the victory?
What has been lost?

Kernow and Cambria, Erin and Alba –
Logres, alas, Logres …

Fang and wing,
flame and claw –
the dragons of Albion
make war, make war.

Song of the North Wind

Wild North Wind

frosty breath from the broken teeth of glaciers,
breaching spume of sperm whales,
endless stillness of the taiga,
ineffable Fata Morgana of the aurora borealis.

Wild North Wind

unsentimental, austere,
you suffer no fools –
cut the wheat from the chaff,
strip bare all illusions.

Wild North Wind

your howling song sends men bosky,
makes seadogs batten down hatches –
become winter stay-at-homes, hearth-tenders, coal-biters,
nurture the fires of families, recite sagas, nurse grudges.

Wild North Wind

grey-cloaked raider, storm-herder,
all bow to your power –
mightiest of winds, bringer of the white death,
the cold kiss of eternal peace.

Wild North Wind

a grim giant striding the land,
heavy boots on rooftops, dislodging drift –

tile-clatterer, sky-strafer,
son of the midnight sun.

Wild North Wind

when will you stop your restless search for vengeance?
when will you cease your bloodfeud with summer?
when will your tundra heart thaw?

A Steampunk Manifesto

Of pistons and empires
built on imagination, hyperbole and
Morlock sweat
let me speak!

The future is steam, I have seen it come true –
the sky is not the limit!
Let us build railways to the stars –
cantilever bridges across the abyss.

There is nothing we cannot achieve
if we put our hundredmonkeyminds to it.
Simian Shakespeares,
typing out the unwritten magnum opus
of the new paradigm –
minting tomorrow.

Let the presses roll –
pour your hot lead words
into my waxy ear.
Coin the phrase to unlock the people
from their mental chains.

DIY revolutionaries, tinkering
with the consensus reality –
customizing iconoclasts,
engineering difference.

Throw a spanner in the works
of the status quo. Break
from the patent, mass-produced mediocrity.

A pox on your plastic paradise –
here's to the new epoch!
The future is steam –
pull the lever and live your dream!

Let us talk
of cogs and corsets,
of mole machines and airships,
naphtha lamps and aethernauts,
bombastic barons and
mechanical Mata Haris.

Show me your bling
and I'll show you mine.
Copper epaulettes and
brass basques, finely fitted
waistcoats and pocket compasses –
pointing in one direction –
backwards into the future!

Brush the velvet of your stiff black hat,
polish the amber lenses of your goggles,
step up to the plate
of your insane machine
and blow your whistle –
yesterday's future is ours!

Equinox Bridge

Rising to the brightening fields
to the bridge of day and night –
where all is in balance
briefly.

Friends, families, dog-walkers gather
by the quickening stream –
united by their mutual awe.

This morning a country
holds its breath,
the day of the new moon,
the day of the Spring Equinox,
the day of the solar eclipse,
the sun entering Aries –

all the usual astrological mumbo-jumbo.

But the solar system is not our personal orrery.

The show is not for us,
although we act like it is.

Not full totality here,
but dramatic enough
for us to stand and stare,
astonished,
as the moon takes a bite out of the sun,
Fenris's rabid bite-marks
raising hackles of primal fear
beyond science and common sense.

Birds quieten, a wind stirs,
pets are bewildered.

Yet we know the light will win in the end.

The moon for once
turns its face away
from the radiance.
A loyal mirror
today is shattered.

Some will turn away from goodness;
some will turn away from the light.
Some choose evil's imagined glamour;
some choose the night.

And yet, in the great scheme of things
(has anyone had a look lately?)
both are needed.
Not a fifty-fifty fixed rigidity
but a flowing, a to-ing and fro-ing,
like rough-and-tumble cubs fighting.

Towards summer, the lion of sunlight dominates;
towards winter, a beast cast in night's bronze.

Both have their place in the Great Dance.

Yet often the light feels frail.
Ah,
so much darkness in the world.

Black-clad barbarians enacting their
impotent rage on aid workers,
schoolchildren, museum visitors.
Infantile despots wanting the world

to comply with their solipsistic
cyclopean monomania –
their pinhead paradigm,
which perverts its own doctrines
to serve whatever devil lurks inside.

See them nurse their grievance narratives,
polish their Russian rifles,
strap on their home-made bombs –
thinking their lonely library of a single book
can justify destroying all others.

Yet this morning all of that is erased
by the sublime benediction of the new sun,
still shining its endless love on all of its children.

This morning the Earth is like a prayer –
grass, flower, tree: hands raised in praise.
All that lives, that is truly alive,
turns towards the light.

So, I stand,
one foot in the shade
one foot in the light –
between the Horns and the Heavens,
a balancing act, a tightrope walk,
across the Niagaras of positive and negative,
moving stubbornly beyond duality.
Beyond a binary world of
with-us or against-us.

Poised on Equinox Bridge,
knowing as I cross it
that it disappears behind me as I pass,
that it never truly existed –

a fleeting moment, a pulse of awareness,
cherry blossom falling on snow.

And somewhere the future
is surging towards us like the swell of the bore;
and somewhere a king
with a black name is buried;
and somewhere Persiled druids
stand posing in the sun.

All bathed in
eight-minute-old light
scattering photons
magnanimously across the tilting Earth,
the part we call north,
the place we call home

in the blink of a blind god's eye.

Walking to Maia

Walking to stillness, walking to wind-through-the-dry-grass,
to estuary emptiness, the Solway at low tide,
skirl of a lonely gull, tang of salt and seaweed,
lap-lap on mudflats, a dog licking its wounds.

I'm walking to Maia, away from Maya.

Walking away from the bullshit,
walking away from the banks,
walking away from Westminster,
from the politicans' self-interested dance.
Walking away from the rolling news bombardment,
vomiting violence 24/7,
making us fear the other,
fear our neighbour
and feed the cycle
that sells the news,
sells the guns, sells the bombs,
sells the panic rooms, the state-of-the-art tombs.

I'm walking to Maia, away from Maya.

Walking away from the High Street,
everything-must-go-closing-down-forever-two-for-one-75%-
discount-sale.
Walking away from Legoland and Lego people.
Walking away from self-servile stations,
from motorway gridlock toomanycars,
from the littering doggybagshitters in the parks.
From animal sadism
and people masochism,

from zero-hours contracts
and fat-cat bonuses.

I'm walking to Maia, away from Maya.

Walking away from Putin and Netanyahu.
Walking away from ISIS and ebola.
Walking away from everyday sexism and FGM.
Walking away from childhood hero child abuse
and internet porn – its virtual voyeurism that makes it the
norm.
Walking away from the NSA, from GCHQ and hacking hacks.

I'm walking to Maia, I'm walking to Maia.

Along my long straight road
following a wall of will,
to the vanishing point
where I hope the land runs out
before my legs.

Mantra of footstep
And breath. Balancing
Inside the Roman
And the Pict.

Eildon Tree

Words, vibrant as rowanberries,
hang poised for the plucking
from the quickening air.
Here, at the Rhymer's Stone,
worlds meet
and poetry is born.

The sun shines its benedictions down.
A fey breeze stirs the hedgerows.
Two slim trunks entwine like lovers.
A nameless bird sings a nameless song,
is replied to.

Stillness after the city.
Meeting the muse for a coffee,
hoarse from the Fringe,
heartsore from love's disappointments.
She points me the way in the battered atlas,
three roads to choose from –
cairn or kirk or loch.

Roots snake deep into the peat,
draw up the sap of inspiration
conjured from the alchemy of
sunlight, rain, wind and night.

I lie like Thomas of Ercildoun on Huntlie Bank,
and the Queen of Elfland rides into view –
a woman cyclist in her Lycra and helmet,
exchanging a bit of banter with two old characters
about the secrets of the gates
known only to them.

Beneath the Eildons' three peaks –
split it is said by a demon that
that old wizard Michael Scot confounded,
still to this day failing to make rope
from the sands of the Tweed –
the magical and the mundane rub shoulders.
The upper and lower get acquainted.

Climb up behind the Queen.
Let her guide you to her hidden kingdom.
The jingle of her rein sends you into a trance –
long hair coiling, blood lips enticing,
the tendrils of her song
piercing your heart.

Follow her siren call
to the end of all that you know.

Be prepared to not be
the same upon your return.

The Corvine Tree

Late 1618: as he sat under the Corvine Tree (the 'Company Tree'), a sycamore that once stood in front of his home, Hawthornden Castle, the poet William Drummond greeted the playwright Ben Johnson, who was walking from London to Edinburgh: 'Welcome, welcome, Royal Ben!' Johnson replied, 'Thank ye, thank ye, Hawthornden!'

Blow your hardest, winds of the world;
Time's river tumbles near.
Howl against Hawthornden's high walls,
skirling Esk's steady roar.

By the ruinous tower proud,
within famed halls austere,
bards gather weary from hard road
to face the great work sheer.

Scaling the cliffs of effort stark,
free-climbing heights alone,
the torch of wit alights the dark,
makes whisper loud mute stone.

From compass's crossroad they come;
for a moon's wheel they dwell,
leaving lover, kin, known and home,
in snug, isolate cell.

Entering the caves of the mind,
dungeons of the unsaid,
wrestling with angels, de'ils, mankind,
within the page, the bed.

Gather for feasts, for talk, for cheer.
Share the tale and the toil.
By hearth, by platter, they draw near,
in wood, chapel and soil.

Clock ticks, pen scratch, keyboard tap-tap,
the pages stack, files stored,
amid tomes leaf turns, ink saps,
day, night, grows the word-hoard.

The black dog lurks and dreams bite deep,
peace, solitude, turn tide;
mundane demands stir us from sleep
as the horn gate swings wide.

Night Running

The trees' quicksilver circuitry
wires my brain to run –
to pull on gear with illicit thrill.
My fitness bid a midnight flit –
hi-viz, Petzl, mud-branded pumps,
but no smug smartwatch
recording the GPS pulse of my route.
I'm going analogue,
off-grid, incommunicado,
following the way of the fox.
Headphoneless, I'm all ears
as a nocturnal impulse impels me
down darkling lanes, clocking
holloways of black and silver,
the spilt ink of naked branches,
mother-of-pearl membrane of cirrocumulus.

I gravitate to the industrial
thrum of the weir,
forge of swan down,
curve of crossbow neck
beneath the stern Victorian frown
of the cartoon-daubed viaduct,
arches like black angels
mantling their wings
over the cracked souls of derelicts.

Trains thunder by, a stampede of light,
as I push the LED cone before me,
a block of pale prayer
strapped to my brow,
winking in agreement with the

strange blink in the sky,
a satellite solidarity.

Running contra to the drunken tide,
riding high on holier-than-thou fumes –
until I pratfall down rubbled jitties,
curse barked to the harkening darkness.
A badger swaggers by in his burglar's mask
disturbing bins – out on his night run too,
his a survival imperative, not an exercise fad.

Back home, the feral blood
sings in my ears.

I bring the night inside.

Walking to the Light

We strike out at dead of night,
old friends, recognizing
each other in the dark.
The midnight chimes fade as we
follow canals Martian in thin beams,
push up the unforgiving hill,
measured by breath,
out on to the trackless common
navigating by hope,
the crump of a dark herd.

Hot from our efforts,
drink tea in our T-shirts at 2 a.m.
Ahead through the woods,
fireflies, fairies, UFOs?
No, blinking roadwork lanterns,
tired eyes playing tricks.
Through the spectral beechwood
we pause, kill our headtorches. Listen.

Drink in the night.

Stumble on, clown-footed with fatigue,
we reach our zenith in the darkest hour,
huddled inside Nympsfield Long Barrow's
broken-toothed remains like bog bodies.
The last of the flask, then a dry push
back. A break in the trees, sublime sky,
twilight of the Lover and the Warlord
cupped by a crescent moon. Dawn's nimbus
a promise of redemption for the benighted world.

Standing mute in wonder like Stone Age men
we witness the sun's orb rise
full over Selsley Barrow, reforged,
moment of ancient glory ever young.

We have made it. We all can
while friends help each other
through the dark,
guide companions to the light
by the star we all carry
and sometimes let others glimpse.

The Slumbering Bard

Spine against the vertebrae
of the Pennines,
legs heavy with hundreds of miles
of heavy metal riding
stretch to the south,
to Cornwall's blistered coast,
feet cooling in the memory of Ys,
sun-brown arms stretch out
across the Marches and the Fens,
one hand on Cader Idris,
the other, the Wash,
unburdened shoulders rest upon
the green bosom of the Dales,
Shining Tor my solar plexus,
a crown of stars above my wild bed,
the calm blanket of night
swaddling my dreams.
I sigh into the soil, still
after many days' motion.
Let England hold me –
body if not mind,
my head in the ptarmigan-plumed
summits of the Highlands yet,
the long deep mirror of Lomond,
the unfallen world caught in its
grey glass. My echo still ringing
in the noble Glens, the paths of song,
droving me home.

The Battle of Brunanburh

Athelstan, king, lord of the war-host,
giver of rings, with his blood-friend
Edmund, prince, won glory eternal
in the fray with their swift sword-talk.

Round Brunanburh
they broke the board-wall,
fought for their land, its hoards and homes,
against the foes' frenzy.

Toppled their opponents,
the Scottish warriors and pirate host –
fey they fell to earth.

The field of battle,
blood-dark at sunrise
with soldiers' gore.
A glorious star rose,
God's bright candle,
passed across the plains,
sank to slumber, set.

It saw the fallen
strewn across the fields.
Northman, spear-marred,
Scotsman, axe-tired,
Hibernian, still.

The best of Wessex
did not slacken,
pressed on their heels,

harried the fleeing host
with stone-keen barbs.

Athelstan's men refused
hard battleplay to none
among the fighters
who with Anlaf came
over roiling surf
bringing invasion's wave
crashing to these shores.

Wyrd spoke their fate –
five young kings
crow-meat upon the battlefield,
by cruel swords kissed
to dreamless sleep.

And more, and more,
Anlaf's earls, seven be told,
and numberless others
of the Scot and the sea dog.

The Northmen's chief –
put to flight,
by dire need driven
with his band to seek his prow.
Sliding across the shingle, with dragon bow
a king departed
on the precious flood.
His royal life preserved
if not his pride.

Old Constantinus, that wily veteran,
escaped too, to his northland
fled; ashamed he watched
the wake, salt-wounded by

friends lost. Lacking kin
in the battle's embrace.

His son forsaken
hacked down
to die in that slaughter-pit.

Grey-maned father bereft –
little cause had he
to brag of that battle
on the mead bench.
And no laughter for Anlaf either.
No boastings or ale songs
with old comrades wrapped in winter's cloak.

When banners clashed
on the field of testing
spears spoke,
hero hailed hero
with hate,
iron-tongued
war banter was all
with Edward's heirs
upon the carnage ground.

In their iron-nailed ships
the Norsemen retreated,
sorrow's survivors,
arrow-haired
on Dingesmere harrowed.
Over the deep whale road
back to Black Town,
to Erin with hearts of lead.

Triumphant, the brothers
to royal hearth returned, helms high.

King and prince to friendly hills
home, horse-proud.
Shield to shield, scabbard to scabbard,
their men marched to the meads of Wessex,
singing victory songs.

For shadows, they left
bloated corpses
for that black-cloaked croaker,
the flesh-stabber, eye-piercer,
to glut upon.
And for snow-winged, earth-breasted
eagle, for greedy warhawk
and drawling forest wolf,
a feast.

Nor has there on this rough-girdled island
ever yet been a greater number tithed,
harvested by the sword's scythe
too early, a bitter grain.

As the chronicles relate,
and wise and withered scholars,

then hither came
the Angles and Saxons
from the cold-breathed east
over the broad grey sea,
envious of this land of ours,
peacebreakers, warmakers,
droving the Britons west,
seizing this sundered isle,
a kingdom for the taking.

As the chronicles relate.

Invocation to Brighid

Hail Brighid,
welcome back into our lives, bright goddess!
Bring the whiteness of the swan's wing.
Bring the softness of the candle's flame.
Bring the ogee of adder's sliding spine.
Bring the pale kisses of snowdrops on the brow of dawn.
Bring the wild laughter of children into our homes.
Bring the sword of light in defence of the vulnerable.
Bring the grace and wisdom of women into the halls of men.
Bring iron, sweat and fire to the forge of words.

The Hallows

Four Hallows before me
Four Hallows behind me
Four Hallows above me
Four Hallows below me

Sword of Light sheathed in city Gorias,
Uscias protects in the place of Bright Battle.
Spear of Lugh held in city Findias,
by Esrus the Kindler tended, warden of skill.
Cauldron of Dagda seated in city Murias,
by Semias guarded, defender of art.
Stone of Fail stands proud in city Falias,
held by Morfessa, on hill of High Kings,
holdfast of knowledge.

By Sword and Spear, Cauldron and Stone I am protected.
By Sword and Spear, Cauldron and Stone I am powerful.
By Sword and Spear, Cauldron and Stone I am complete.

Deep Peace

Deep peace of the glens be with you
Deep peace of the lochs be with you
Deep peace of the hills be with you
Deep peace of the burns be with you
Deep peace of the woods be with you
Deep peace of the green lanes be with you
Deep peace of the day's hollows be with you
Deep peace of the summer dusk be with you
Deep peace of the night's harbour be with you

as you walk in the love of the land.

Notes on the Poems

Blessings of the Silver Branch
I used to use this to open my performances back when I performed as 'Tallyessin' (my bardic stage name when I first started out).

I Am, My Dear Mary
One of my very first published poems, printed in *Stealing Ivy*, an anthology of Northampton Poets, and performed during the John Clare bicentenary in 1992 at venues around the town, including the portico of All Saints' Church where Clare used to hand out poems to passers-by.

The Bard's Prayer
A very early poem (1993), which I remember reading to my girlfriend's mum when she asked me for a poem. Lord knows what she made of me after that!

The Child of Everything
Written in the late 1990s when the anti-GMO movement was in full swing. Using the anamorphic poems of Taliesin as a springboard, I enjoyed updating the metaphors. I performed spontaneously from memory in Trafalgar Square in front of thousands of people during an anti-GMO march. Halfway through I heard my amplified voice booming out across the crowds and nearly lost my nerve – but I kept going and got away with it, just!

Thirty
Performed at the launch of the anthology it was part of – *Generations* (2000) – in a launch showcase in Bristol alongside fellow contributors.

Phone Tree
I often use this as a warm-up, making a joke about audiences 'leaving their phones turned *on* for its duration' before politely asking them to ensure their phones are off.

Roaming Home
Performed at open mike events after my return from a nine-month odyssey around South East Asia in the mid 1990s.

The Ruin
This is my reconstruction of an eighth-century poem inspired by the remains of Aquae Sulis (Roman Bath), probably written by a visiting Saxon cleric, and surviving on a piece of badly burnt parchment in Exeter Cathedral. 'Wyrd' is the Anglo-Saxon concept of fate. I've performed it many times over the years – in storytelling shows and, in situ, as part of my Bard of Bath Tour.

*Bio*Wolf*
Written with performance in mind, my cyberpunk version of *Beowulf* was premiered in the Bardic Festival of Bath, 1999, in a Saxon-themed showcase also featuring Kirsty Hartsiotis and Widsith the Scop. I learnt it by heart and found performing it an intense, visceral performance.

Spring Fall
Premiered at 'Enchanted Wood: A Celebration of the Spirit of Nature', Bath Fringe 1998, with my then partner, Emily Tavakoly, this long poem won me the Bardic Chair of Caer Badon to make me the Third Bard of Bath. The main poem is often performed in conjunction with 'The Solace of Sulis' and 'Awakening the King'. I've also performed the latter at several events celebrating the mythic king of Bath.

The Bride of Spring
Performed at pretty much every Imbolc (31 January/1 February) since I wrote it in 1991.

The Wheel of the Rose
Commissioned and performed for my friends, Stephen and Hannah Isaac, for their wedding at Comlongon Castle, Scotland. It's been handy whenever love has been in the air, e.g. a handfasting at St Briavel's Castle, Forest of Dean, Midsummer 2017.

Birds of Rhiannon
Turned into a lovely song by my old Bath friend Rae, who performed it with guitar.

Merry Maiden
Inspired by a beautiful spring walk along the South West Coastal Path through Lamorna Cove. I started out attempting to sing this in a failed band back in Northampton, appropriately called 'F'.

The Winning of Spring
Created in my '*Mabinogion* phase' (i.e. obsession) and often performed in the Beltane season.

Maid Flower Bride
This poem went down particularly well when I performed it one year at the Bardic Finals of Ynys Witrin, Glastonbury. I often perform this poem in conjunction with my retelling of the story 'Llew Llaw Gyffes'.

One with the Land
Probably my most performed poem since I composed it in 1991. It has been performed at many pagan (and non-pagan) events in Britain and America.

Heart Wood
Created for *Robin of the Wildwood*, a show co-created with other members of Fire Springs, this poem was turned into a beautiful song by Rachel Shurmer, played with harp accompaniment, and has been a tried-and-trusted friend whenever a bit of enchantment is called for.

In the Name of the Sun

Written for the Summer Solstice and performed most memorably on my Stonehenge Tours (on a coach leaving the Stonehenge visitor centre, after an all-nighter to and from London).

Praise Song for a Lost Festival

Performed in the Poetry and Words Tent, Glastonbury, and generally in the summer when Pilton is on.

Ancestral Mariner

Performed during story shows about the Manx deity – so quite niche!

Last Orders for John Barleycorn

Premiered at an event I organised as a fundraiser for Lowdown, a Young People's Advisory Service in Northampton. I performed the poem with musical accompaniment from Dominic Reid-Jones and Andy Clayson (calling ourselves 'Triptych'). I recall ripping apart a loaf at the poem's climax.

Summer's Wake

Written for the Autumn Equinox, 1991, and performed on many occasions since at that time of year.

The Enchantment of Merlin

Written for *Arthur's Dream*, the first show created by Fire Springs (back then comprising the founder members: Anthony Nanson, Kirsty Hartsiotis, David Metcalfe and myself).

Wild Hunt

Performed in *Robin of the Wildwood* – particularly resonant at the premiere, on 1 May 2002, at Rocks East Woodland, against the backdrop of the hundred-acre wood lovingly managed by the late great Tony Philips, the quintessential old man of the woods.

Wolf in the City

This one often feels quite edgy, but I love channelling my inner wolf.

The Wicker Man

Performed in front of a full-sized wicker man at the Mercian Gathering as it went up in flames. Dramatic!

The Battle for the Trees

Performed as part of *Robin of the Wildwood* with help from Anthony Nanson and Kirsty Hartsiotis.

All Heal

Performed at pretty much every Yuletide since I composed it in celebration of the magical plant – most memorably at the Tenbury Mistletoe Festival.

Heather's Spring

Written for a friend suffering from cancer. I have since spoken this piece at the bedside of other dying friends. Almost unbearable to think about, but it does seem to have a profound effect upon the listener.

The Prophet of Los

Performed alongside my much-missed old poet friend Simon Miles in Tate Britain and Tate Modern on William Blake's birthday (28 November). We managed to get ejected from the latter's premises by security when they objected to our impromptu 'art action' in the forecourt: Simon tearing pages out of his folder and scattering them around me in a magical circle as I declaimed it. As a Dadaism/Surrealism exhibition was on at the time, we thought it was entirely appropriate!

Sunrise Praise

Inspired by a Seneca prayer, I decided to create my own 'morning praise song' and this is what I came up with. It is lovely to way to greet the new day, dew wet on your bare feet.

Dragon Dance

This long poem was commissioned by the artist Beth Townley for a performance piece. I turned it into a chapbook and have been honoured to witness it being performed in a ceremony at Stonehenge by the Cotswold Pagan Society (with different groups reciting each section). I have also perform it myself in different parts of England, Wales, Ireland and Scotland – a powerful way to honour the spirit of the land.

The Taliesin Soliloquies

I wrote this long sequence for *The Way of Awen: Journey of a Bard* (O Books, 2010) and I have performed its constituent poems as part of my 'Way of Awen' playshop at the Minerva Centre, Bath. 'The Creation of Taliesin', however, was written in the late 1990s and I have performed it many times, either by itself or as part of my telling of Taliesin's creation myth. Many of the Penbeirdd's poems are gnomic and obscure, but, as with the *Mabonogion*, I have found that by using my own words I forge a way in and the mysteries reveal themselves. Whenever I perform this poem, I feel filled with Taliesinic energy; it is a powerful portal into the awen. 'Cerddeu' = 'poems'. 'Cariad' = 'love'.

Prayer for Awen

This is another one of my 'portable portals': as an invocation it does the job.

Born of the People's Strength

My praise song to the town of my birth. Performing this at the Bardic Picnic one year, in Delapré Abbey, felt especially resonant. It is a kind of summoning and a counter-charm to break the sleep spell that seemed to dwell over the town when I was growing up there. Its title comes from the Saxon saint, Ragener, whose tomb was found in the remarkable Norman church of St Peter's, Marefair.

The Green Abbey

A praise song in honour of a place very special to me, the former Clunaic Nunnery of Delapré Abbey and its wilderness gardens where I walked my dog every day when I was growing up just over the

London Road. I also performed this at the Bardic Picnic, and it felt very moving to honour the genius loci in this way. Words of beauty and gratitude, spoken in situ, can have a powerful resonance. It is a kind of reciprocation.

Memory Wood
Written in honour of another special place – Rocks East Woodland, which became my new 'Delapré' when I moved to Bath and discovered the place in a newspaper article likening it to something out of Middle Earth. If you know Puzzle Wood in the Forest of Dean, Rocks East has a similar vibe. I became poet-in-residence there during my year as Bard of Bath, and organized several events there, including the Lost Forest and Wild Wood camps. The poem was my way of saying thanks to the woods and to the late Tony Philips, its owner and guardian, who allowed me to flourish there.

Cooildarry
Inspired by a numinous place on the Isle of Man, this poem was written with the euphonic effect at the forefront of my mind. I am fascinated by place names – their incantatory quality.

On Malvern Hills
Inspired by the lovely Malverns and designed to be recited from its heights.

On Ventry Sands
Poems can capture an experience better than any photograph – in a holistic, 360-degree way. This one was inspired by a cove on the Dingle Peninsula where I found the Finn stone amidst playful dolphins and the *Fisherman's Blues.* (The classic *Fisherman's Blues* album by the Waterboys was recorded in the area.)

Prydwen and the Cauldron
Written for performance at the opening ceremony of the annual Wessex Gathering on the Isle of Purbeck – a feat of memory and nerve in front of a circle of three hundred people.

The Red Lady

Inspired by the remarkable (and difficult to access) Paviland Cave, on the Gower Peninsula – the neck of the woods of the neglected Swansea-based bard Vernon Watkins, whose Taliesinic poetry haunts its coves and crags.

The Chair of the Sea

Ynys Enlli, the Island of Currents, is the Welsh name for Bardsey. The island is a pilgrimage place of significance (three trips to Ynys Enlli was the equivalent of a trip to Rome in medieval 'God-miles'). The first time I went there was to take part in a Whale and Dolphin Conservation Society survey; the second time, on solo retreat. I hope to go back again one day to the Isle of Bards. Môna was the druids' name for Anglesey; Eyri, the old name of Snowdon.

Thirteen Treasures

The 'Thirteen Treasures of Britain' are mentioned in several historical sources, including the Welsh Triads. I wanted to create a poem that encoded them in a memorable way. I performed it at the Wessex Gathering one year in the opening ceremony.

House of the Moon

Inspired by the unique, bosky, brilliant and sadly defunct 'Castle of the Muses', on Loch Goil, once home of the 'peace druid', Dr Thomas Daffern, and stuffed to the ginnels with his massive library. Each room was dedicated to a muse – although the muses were somewhat crowded out by Thomas's toppling bookshelves. I performed the full poem on my final night there as a way of praising the Muses, mine host and the colourful guests he attracted. Mnemosyne was the Goddess of Memory and mother of the Muses. Her name means 'House of the Moon'.

Moon Bathing

Inspired by my final, wild night in El Gouna, Egypt – a resort on the Red Sea where I spent a month as writer-in-residence, working on my fourth Windsmith novel, *The Burning Path.* I've enjoyed performing it at the Skyros 'cabaret' – a tradition on the Skyros Writers' Lab holidays I've tutored on a few times. My ode to late-night skinny-dipping always seems to go down well.

Looking Back
My poem about Orpheus and Eurydice was performed as part of the Fire Springs show *Return to Arcadia.*

Your Love
In *Song of the Windsmith*, the multimedia extravaganza I co-created with musical maestro James Hollingsworth to promote the Windsmith Elegy novels in 2012, this poem was performed with the accompaniment of music and, on one memorable occasion, live belly dancing.

Breaking Light
First published in *Soul of the Earth: the awen anthology of eco-spiritual poetry* (2011), edited by Jay Ramsay, and performed at the launch of this book in Waterstones, Bath, in front of my friends.

The Secret Commonwealth
This set of ten poems are part of a fictional 'album' I created for Janey McEttrick, my protagonist in *The Knowing – A Fantasy.* The album is called *The Secret Commonwealth* after her ancestor Robert Kirk's monograph, *The Secret Commonwealth of Elves, Fauns and Fairies* (1691). I tried to learn guitar as part of my experiential research for this project and these songs were my first attempts at composing, singing and playing my own material.

The Three Sisters
Turned into a beautiful song on harp by Chantelle Smith.

Crows in the Willows
This is one of my earliest songs. It featured in *Green Fire* (2004) and then was requisitioned for Janey's album.

Blood Red Moon
Performed beautifully as a song by my friend Nimue Brown.

Follow the Sun Road Home
This poem too was published in *Green Fire* and also included in *The Secret Commonwealth.* I remember performing it one New Year's Eve at a party given Daisy Blake in her father Peter Blake's old chapel studio, Wellow, near to Stoney Littleton Long Barrow.

Dragons of War
Performed as part of *Song of the Windsmith* with fiery musical magic by James Hollingsworth. A performance in Bath Masonic Hall stands out in memory.

A Steampunk Manifesto
Performed as part of the warm-up for *Song of the Windsmith.* I recall looning around Bath in full costume with James Hollingsworth ('Merlin') and Miriam Schaffer ('Aveldra' and 'Amelia'), reciting this as we promoted our show in the Fringe. Also performed at Asylum.

Equinox Bridge
Performed at Richard Austin's *Feast of Friends*, Star Anise Arts Cafe, Stroud, on 10 April 2015.

Walking to Maia
Performed in the Cheltenham Poetry Festival with Chantelle Smith in a set entitled *Across the Lost Border.* Maia is the name of the last Roman fort on Hadrian's Wall, at Bowness-on-Solway, eighty-four miles from Wallsend, the start of our walk in 2014.

The Corvine Tree
Performed at Jay Ramsay's birthday celebration, Hawkwood College, 2016. The quatrains mirror the Corvine Tree's other name: 'the Four Sisters'.

Night Running
Inspired by one of my nocturnal habits.

Walking to the Light
Inspired by a 'midnight to dawn' walk I undertook one midsummer with my old friend Anthony Nanson.

The Battle of Brunanburh
Created for a ballad and tale show, *Flight of a Sparrow*, performed with my partner, Chantelle Smith, at Malmesbury Abbey library during their Wessex Week – that year celebrating the life of Athelstan.

Invocation to Brighid
Performed at Stroud Out Loud Imbolc Showcase, 4 February 2018.

The Hallows
Composed and performed as part of the Bríghíd's Flame show *The Hallows*, premiered on 24 June 2017 at St Briavels Castle, in the Forest of Dean, during the 'Tales of Witchcraft and Wonder' weekend.

Deep Peace
Performed on Swift's Hill, near Stroud, in July 2017, at a friend's birthday picnic, upon my return from walking the 212 miles of the Southern Upland Way.

The Shining Word

He whose face gives no light will never be a star.

William Blake

Make your performance shine with this five-point method:

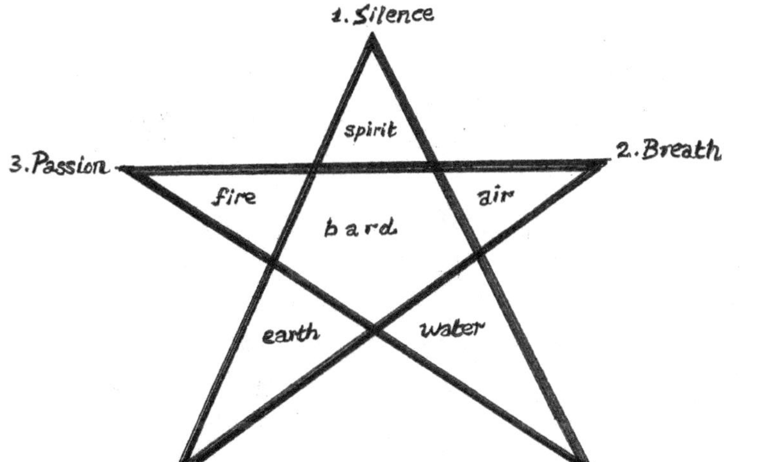

1. *Silence.* Listen to your heart, to the Earth, to Spirit, to the universe. What does it want you to say? Meditate. Invoke the awen and ask for inspiration. Consider the Endless Sound: the silence between the words.
2. *Breath.* Breathe from below (your diaphragm). Warm up the vocal

chords with voice exercises, e.g. humming, toning, chanting. Take deep breaths to relax and to keep your lungs filled. Speak slowly and clearly. Project.

3. *Fire in the heart.* Speak from the heart and say it loud and proud, with passion, with sincerity, with energy, but do not 'scorch'! Temper with …
4. *Ripples in the pond.* After passion comes compassion. Be sensitive to your audience, your words and yourself. Imagine dropping pebbles in a pond with your words: let each one have its impact. Be aware of the energy you are raising, the atmosphere you are creating.
5. *Bring it down to earth.* Make sure your message reaches home by manifesting it fully. Use body language, movement, props, costume, drums. Establish and use the space. Use humour and spontaneity. Take the audience on a magical healing journey there and back again.

The Cauldron Born

Stories offer us an insight into the mysteries of this land, or wherever they originate. Knowing the tales of a place helps us to access its genius loci and the psyche of its people. They let us get under the skin, and they get under our skin – working on our subconscious through the language of dreams, bypassing logic to access wisdom.

So it is with the Welsh cycle of stories known as the *Mabinogion.* Recorded by monks in the twelfth or thirteenth century, but dating back far earlier, they are a body of teachings from the native tradition, miraculously surviving the ravages of time and man – by hiding in plain sight as a bunch of 'harmless' tales for the young. Yet within them are contained bizarre and dark images, brutal truths, and archetypes unmitigated by political correctness. Primal and powerful, these stories may at times seem raw, crude or convoluted – but, like

Chinese whispers, they had been told many times before being transcribed by monks with perhaps little inkling of their original significance. What we get is a degenerated copy of the original, but by meditating upon the symbolism it is possible to tap into the inner teachings and consequently enjoy the tales with fresh insight.

For me, the tale of Taliesin was the key that unlocked these mysteries. It was the first tale I told as a story – without script, on request, at an Arthurian party: my first bardic commission. It became my 'signature tale' as I connected more and more to the lore and legend of Taliesin. He was the master bard and I was his apprentice. I strive to honour his name and what he stands for: the bardic tradition of Britain. Although this tradition has druidic roots, I see it as non-denominational and of use to people of all paths. It is about speaking with spirit – saying what you mean and meaning what you say, making sacred the air. It is gramarye – word magic. You can use it to cast a spell or circle, to hold a ceremony or celebration, to bless, curse, seduce and heal. But, as with all magic, bear in mind the three-fold effect. Words are powerful things, to be used wisely, carefully and sensitively. I would not advise using words to curse, or to impart any negativity. I once incorporated a curse into a short story – which won me the Bath Ghost Story Prize, but got pulled from the local newspaper for being too controversial!

A bard does not have to have a beard. Or play a harp. He or she can be a storyteller, poet or musician, although traditionally the bard was all these things, as well as genealogist, journalist, historian – in short, a walking library! A bard's training would take twelve to twenty years, depending on the school, and the bard would be expected to learn 350 tales by the end. In modern times, although I encourage people to remember and perform their material, rather than read it out, I would suggest that anyone who uses the sacred word to entertain and enchant is a bard of sorts. But, in all modesty, I don't think being a bard is something you can claim for yourself. The proof of the pudding is whether folk like what you do, are willing to listen and, better still, invite you back to do more. If you are fulfilling that niche in a tribe, clan, coven, order, moot or any other kind of community, then you are bard of that community.

Yet I encourage everyone to have a go at storytelling or performance poetry. Try it out at local open mike. Story circles have sprung up all around the country and are great sharing spaces, whatever your faith or path.

Taliesin walks between the worlds, inhabiting like King Arthur both history and myth. There was a sixth-century Welsh bard called Taliesin, whose praise poems to his lord are still extant. Then there is the Taliesin of legend, with his own creation myth – the archetypal shaman-bard, who journeyed with Arthur into the Underworld to win the fabled cauldron of plenty. Yet it was from 'another' cauldron – ultimately, all cauldrons are one, as one chalice represents *the* Chalice – the Cauldron of Inspiration, that Taliesin received his poetic gift. It belonged to Ceridwen, the wisest woman in Wales, the witches' witch …

Ceridwen had given birth to an ill-favoured son, Afaggdu. To compensate for his ugliness, the Woman of the Craft decided to concoct a potion of inspiration for him. She collected the ingredients and cooked them in her cauldron. She got Gwion Bach, a boy from the nearby village, to stir the cauldron, and an old man to stoke the fire – for a year and a day. Alas, when the task was nearly complete, Gwion became sleepy and dropped in the spoon – splashing his hand. He quickly put his burnt fingers in his mouth and – eureka! – received the distilled wisdom meant for Afaggdu. The rest of the potion was poisonous, and split the cauldron. Gwion knew Ceridwen would have his guts for garters – so he hightailed it out of there, in the form of a hare. With the potion coursing through his veins he had the power to shape-change! So off he dashed, but when Ceridwen discovered the disaster she changed herself into a greyhound and gave chase. Soon she was snapping at his heels, so Gwion jumped into a stream, his fur fell away and he turned in a fish. Ceridwen would not be outwitted and turned herself into a otter-bitch. She had almost caught him, when he leapt into the air, the scales fell away to reveal feathers – he had become a wren, king of the birds. But the sky would not protect him from Ceridwen, who turned from otter to hawk. In a flash she had him within an inch of his life, so Gwion became smaller – a germ of wheat and fell down to the threshing floor of a farmyard. Hawk-eyed Ceridwen dropped down too and became a hen. She plucked Gwion up in her beak and swallowed him.

Nine months later she gave birth to a baby boy so beautiful she could not kill him. But because of ugly Afaggdu she could not keep him, for the boy shone with the wisdom meant for him. So Ceridwen wrapped him up in leather and cast him out on the sea in a coracle. It was May Eve now and Elphin was out fishing at a weir. He wasn't having much luck, and was just about to give up when he spotted the coracle. He pulled it ashore and was astounded to see something move in it. He unwrapped the bundle, saw the baby boy and cried, 'Behold, the Shining Brow!' And that was how Taliesin got his name. The boy shone with an intelligence beyond his years, and immediately began to prophesy good fortune for Elphin and his family. And so, wisely, Elphin took the child home to show Gywddno, his father, and he was adopted.

With Taliesin's praeternatural knowledge, Elphin and his father prospered. One day, at the court of his uncle, King Maelgwyn, Elphin drunkenly boasted he had a bard better than any there. He was clapped in irons for his insolence and the boy-bard was sent for – now thirteen in body. Taliesin came and pitted his wits against the court bards, winning the bardic duel by setting a riddle none could answer. Elphin's claim being vindicated, Elphin was released from the dungeon, and then released Taliesin from his service. He was a bard to great for one man: he belonged to the nation, and so Taliesin became the Royal Bard of Camelot and the greatest bard Albion has ever known.

This amazing story offers us an insight into the bardic mysteries. Like all good stories, it works through symbolism and is worth meditating upon. Taliesin, as Gwion Bach, is the initiate. Ceridwen, a form of the White Goddess no less, is the initiator. He drinks of her cauldron, enters her and becomes 'twice-born' (in Christian terms 'born again'). The awakened Taliesin receives the Shining Brow – the star of his opened third eye, as we all can, by asking for awen. This can be done by chanting 'awen' three times and imagining your third eye opening. Shine and you will be a star!

We can all be Cauldron Born and sup of its inspiration by reading these old tales or, better still, listening to storytellers tell them. From visiting the ancient sites and landscape associated with them I find the stories come alive. From taking the journey you may discover new stories along the way. We take from the pot and add to it anew. Like the three Celtic Cauldrons of Plenty, Inspiration and Rebirth, it fills us with spiritual nourishment, awen and healing.

Performance Poetry Tips

1. Find the fire in your head – the spark to set the poem alight.
2. Use rhyme, rhythm and alliteration as mnemonic devices.
3. Say it out loud until it 'scans to the ear.'
4. Consider what is the core emotion or message. Does it come across?
5. Keep it simple; complication leads to alienation. Be clever between the lines. Communication is about being understood – and that's up to you.
6. Listen to the audience. Let the silences speak.
7. Remember the effort spent crafting your words. Don't throw them away. Speak them with respect. Say them like they're newly minted.
8. Don't undersell yourself, apologise or mumble your words.
9. Keep preambles to a minimum. Cut them out altogether if possible. Go in with a bang!
10. Look sharp and sound sharp. Dress to impress. Wear your confidence overcoat.
11. Remember to breathe! Don't speak too fast … Pause … Let the audience in.
12. Make eye contact as much as possible.
13. Learn your words off by heart if possible. It's more entertaining and more impressive. Audiences appreciate the time and effort

spent learning your words.

14. Passion transcends ability, but honing your craft can only help.
15. Sincerity shines through. Take your efforts seriously and others will too. But humour wins over an audience and circumvents the hecklers.
16. Use body language consciously. Practise your stage presence.
17. If you use a persona, remain fully present and real.
18. Get there early. Practise in the space if possible. Warm up your voice before you start.
19. Practise with microphone if using a PA, or projecting if not. Soundcheck.
20. Use the performance space. Be aware of the energy of the room and audience.
21. Performing poetry is a buzz – enjoy it. Stand up there and shine!

Performance Poetry Devices

- Alliteration
- Dialect/slang
- Group performance
- Humour – it can be simply in the voice, even if the subject is serious
- Imagery
- Multimedia – video projection, audio loops, installations
- Music – either live instruments or backing track
- Persona
- Props
- Repetition/refrain
- Rhetoric
- Rhyme
- Rhythm
- Satire

- Shock – scatalogical language or taboo subjects
- Tone
- Venue – select and make effective use of the venue
- Verbal transformations
- Voice
- Xtravagance! – put on a show with pizzazz!
- Yodelling – only kidding, but practise in a canyon if you can!
- Zen – be fully present – centred, relaxed and aware

Recommended Reading

A.E. (George Russell), *Song and Its Fountains*, Macmillan, New York, 1932.

Blake, William, *The Complete Poems*, Penguin, London, 1978.

Fire Springs, *An Ecobardic Manifesto: A Vision for the Arts in a Time of Environmental Crisis*, Awen, Bath, 2008.

Gersie, Alida, Anthony Nanson & Edward Schiefflin (eds), *Storytelling for a Greener World: Environment, Community, and Story-Based Learning*, Hawthorn Press, Stroud, 2014.

Graves, Robert, *The White Goddess: A Historical Grammar of Poetic Myth*, Faber & Faber, London, 1961.

Hamilton, Claire, *Tales of the Celtic Bards*, O Books, Winchester, 2003.

Hughes, Ted, (ed.), *By Heart: 101 Poems to Remember*, Faber & Faber, London, 1997.

Hughes, Ted, *Winter Pollen: Occasional Prose*, ed. William Scammell, Faber & Faber, London, 1994

Livingstone, Dinah, *The Poetry of Earth*, Katabasis, London, 2000.

Lord, Albert B., *The Singer of Tales*, Atheneum, New York, 1969.

Manwaring, Kevan (ed.), *Ballad Tales*, History Press, Stroud, 2017.

Manwaring, Kevan, *The Bardic Handbook: The Complete Manual for the Twenty-First Century Bard*, Gothic Image, Glastonbury, 2006.

Matthews, Caitlín, *Singing the Soul Back Home: Shamanism in Daily Life*, Element, Shaftesbury, 1995.

Matthews, John (ed.), *The Bardic Source Book: Inspirational Legacy and Teachings of the Ancient Celts*, Blandford, London, 1998.

Matthews, John, *Taliesin: The Last Celtic Shaman,* Rochester, VT: Inner Traditions, 2002.

Motion, Andrew, *Poetry by Heart: A Treasury of Poetry to Be Read Aloud,* Viking, London, 2016.

Opie, Iona & Peter Opie (eds), *Nursery Rhymes*, Oxford University Press, Oxford, 1992.

Raine, Kathleen, *Defending Ancient Springs*, Oxford University Press, London, 1967.

Ramsay, Jay, *Psychic Poetry: A Manifesto*, Diamond Press, London, 1985.

Rilke, Rainer Maria, *Letters to a Young Poet*, trans. Joan M. Burnham, New World Library, San Rafael, CA, 1992

Rilke, Rainer Maria, *The Selected Poetry*, trans. Stephen Mitchell, Picador, London, 1987.

Sampson, Fiona, *The Healing Word,* Poetry Society, London, 1999.

Shaw, Martin, *Branches of the Lightning Tree: Ecstatic Myth and the Grace in Wildness,* White Cloud Press, Ashland, OR, 2011.

Skelton, R. & M. Blackwood (eds), *Earth, Air, Fire, Water*, Arkana, London, 1990.

Stewart, R.J., *Where is Saint George?*, Blandford, London, 1988.

Williamson, Robin, *The Craneskin Bag: Celtic Stories and Poems*, Canongate, Edinburgh, 1989.

Yeats, W.B., *The Collected Poems*, Wordsworth, London, 1994.

Afterword

In an age of post-truth 'fake news' in which discourse is strangled daily by politicians, biased journalism, and bot-generated postings on social media designed to elicit knee-jerk reactions, the re-enchantment of language is needed more than ever. This is not to advocate a fey, magical quality in the way we communicate with one another (something that would quickly become exasperating), but a restoration of meaning – a synchrony of word, intention and action. A return to a more dignified dialogue, not one that is reductive and divisive, triggered and triggering, but one that allows polysemous nuance, subtlety of expression, refinement of argument, criticality and respect. In short, the ennoblement of discourse and the de-commissioning of the weaponised word-armoury that has made almost any public debate a minefield. Those who would divide and rule us hack the frames of our colloquies, dumbing us down to playground name-calling, bullying and tribalism. Saturated with the marketing fodder of kidults, our narratives are arrested – and they have us exactly where they want us. But as the inspiring student-led protests in Parkland, Florida have revealed, it is possible for even the youngest and most vulnerable of society to take back power – echoing mythopoeically what the young Taliesin accomplished in the court of King Maelgwyn. With words of gramarye, well spoken, the strongest of chains can fall away. Let the voices of the disenfranchised be heard and beautiful speech return, and may the awen speak through us all.

Kevan Manwaring

www.awenpublications.co.uk

Also available from Awen Publications:

Soul of the Earth: the Awen anthology of eco-spiritual poetry

edited by Jay Ramsay

Beautifully crafted, yet challenging received wisdom and pushing boundaries, these are cutting-edge poems from a new generation of writers who share a love of the Earth and haven't given up on humans either. In poems as light as a butterfly and as wild as a storm you'll find vivid, contemporary voices that dare to explore a spiritual dimension to life on Earth and, in doing so, imply that a way out of our global crisis of ecological catastrophe, financial meltdown, and bankruptcy of the spirit is to look beyond the impasse of materialism. With contributions from poets in the USA, Canada, UK, Australia, and New Zealand, this anthology reaches out across the planet to embrace the challenges and blessings of being alive on the Earth in the twenty-first century.

'All real poetry seeks to "renew the face of the earth" – and so to resist the exploiting, banalization or defacing of what lies around us. I hope this collection will serve the renewal of vision we so badly need.'
Most Revd Dr Rowan Williams

Poetry ISBN 978-1-906900-17-5 £12.00

The Immanent Moment

Kevan Manwaring

The sound of snow falling on a Somerset hillside, the evanescence of a waterspout on a remote Scottish island, the invisible view from a Welsh mountain, the light on the Grand Canal in Venice, the fire in a Bedouin camel-herder's eyes … These poems consider the little epiphanies of life and capture such fleeting pulses of consciousness in sinuous, euphonic language. A meditation on time, mortality, transience, and place, this collection celebrates the beauty of both the natural and the man-made, the familiar and the exotic, and the interstices and intimacy of love.

Poetry ISBN 978-1-906900-41-0 £8.99

Iona

Mary Palmer

What do you do when you are torn apart by your 'selves'? The pilgrim poet, rebel Mordec and tweedy Aelia set sail for Iona – a thin place, an island on the edge. It's a journey between worlds, back to the roots of their culture. On the Height of Storm they relive a Viking massacre, at Port of the Coracle encounter vipers. They meet Morrighan, a bloodthirsty goddess, and Abbot Dominic with his concubine nuns. There are omens, chants, curses … During her stay Mordec learns that words can heal or destroy, and the poet writes her way out of darkness. A powerful story, celebrating a journey to wholeness, from an accomplished poet.

Poetry ISBN 978-0-9546137-8-5 £6.99 Spirit of Place Volume 1

Mysteries

Chrissy Derbyshire

This enchanting and exquisitely crafted collection by Chrissy Derbyshire will whet your appetite for more from this superbly talented wordsmith. Her short stories interlaced with poems depict chimeras, femmes fatales, mountebanks, absinthe addicts, changelings, derelict warlocks, and persons foolhardy enough to stray into the beguiling world of Faerie. Let the sirens' song seduce you into the Underworld …

Fiction/Poetry ISBN 978-1-906900-45-8 £8.99

Glossing the Spoils

Charlotte Hussey

Each poem in *Glossing the Spoils* works like an intricate time-travel machine, carrying the reader back to the beginnings of Western European literature. Like an ancient clapper bridge with its unmortared slabs of flat sandstone, these poems step us across the choppy currents of the past 1500 years. Anchored at one end in the deep past and at the other in the turbulent present, they explore interconnections between historical, personal, psychological, and mythic states. Plundering their opening passages from such early texts as *Beowulf*, *The Mabinogion*, and *The Tain*, these glosas address eternal themes of love and war and give voice to the surreal potency of the Western European imagination.

Poetry ISBN 978-1-906900-52-6 £8.99

The Long Woman

Kevan Manwaring

An antiquarian's widow discovers her husband's lost journals and sets out on a journey of remembrance across 1920s England and France, retracing his steps in search of healing and independence. Along alignments of place and memory she meets mystic Dion Fortune, ley-line pioneer Alfred Watkins, and a Sir Arthur Conan Doyle obsessed with the Cottingley Fairies. From Glastonbury to Carnac, she visits the ancient sites that obsessed her husband and, tested by both earthly and unearthly forces, she discovers a power within herself.

Fiction ISBN 978-1-906900-44-1 £9.99
The Windsmith Elegy Volume 1

Windsmith

Kevan Manwaring

A man of peace in a time of war, Isambard Kerne must choose between the power of words or swords. The fate of both Earth and its Shadow hangs in the balance. Will he be able to master the Way of the Windsmith in time to save the valley of his ancestors? Or will the terror of war change Kerne into what he fears the most?

Fiction ISBN 978-1-906900-47-2 £9.99
The Windsmith Elegy Volume 2

The Well Under the Sea

Kevan Manwaring

Imagine an island at the crossroads of time where lost souls find each other … Having learnt the secrets of the East Wind, Isambard Kerne must sail beyond the West Wind to the fabled Island of the Blessed, Ashalantë, where the visions of Plato, Da Vinci, and Brunel have come to life. Here he meets the legendary aviatrix Amelia Earhart, who is assigned to instruct him in the art of flying, but they find themselves falling in forbidden love. Torn between duty and desire, the two become embroiled in a tragic chain of events that threaten to destroy not only this otherworldly paradise but also its shadow: Earth.

Fiction ISBN 978-1-906900-48-9 £9.99
The Windsmith Elegy Volume 3

The Firekeeper's Daughter

Karola Renard

From the vastness of Stone Age Siberia to a minefield in today's Angola, from the black beaches of Iceland to the African savannah and a Jewish-German cemetery, Karola Renard tells thirteen mythic stories of initiation featuring twenty-first-century kelpies, sirens, and holy fools, a river of tears and a girl who dances on fire, a maiden shaman of ice, a witch in a secret garden, Queen Guinevere's mirror, and a woman who swallows the moon. The red thread running through them all is a deep faith in life and the need to find truth and meaning even in the greatest of ordeals.

Fiction ISBN 978-1-906900-46-5 £9.99

A Dance with Hermes

Lindsay Clarke

In a verse sequence that swoops between wit and ancient wisdom, between the mystical and the mischievous, award-winning novelist Lindsay Clarke elucidates the trickster nature of Hermes, the messenger god of imagination, language, dreams, travel, theft, tweets, and trading floors, who is also the presiding deity of alchemy and the guide of souls into the otherworld. Taking a fresh look at some classical myths, this vivacious dance with Hermes choreographs ways in which, as an archetype of the poetic basis of mind, the sometimes disreputable god remains as provocative as ever in a world that worries – among other things – about losing its iPhone, what happens after death, online scams, and the perplexing condition of its soul.

Poetry/Mythology ISBN 978-1906900-43-4 £10.00

The Fifth Quarter

Richard Selby

The Fifth Quarter is Romney Marsh, as defined by the Revd Richard Harris Barham in *The Ingoldsby Legends*: 'The World, according to the best geographers, is divided into Europe, Asia, Africa, America and Romney Marsh.' It is a place apart, almost another world. This collection of stories and poems explores its ancient and modern landscapes, wonders at its past, and reflects upon its present. Richard Selby has known Romney Marsh all his life. His writing reflects the uniqueness of The Marsh through prose, poetry, and written versions of stories he performs as a storyteller.

Fiction/Poetry ISBN 978-0-9546137-9-2 £9.99 Spirit of Place Volume 2

Dancing with Dark Goddesses: movements in poetry

Irina Kuzminsky

The dance is life – life is the dance – in all its manifestations, in all its sorrow and joy, cruelty and beauty. And the faces of the Dark Goddesses are many – some are dark with veiling and unknowing, some are dark with sorrow, some are dark with mystery and a light so great that it paradoxically shades them from sight. The poems in this collection are an encounter with many of these faces, in words marked with feminine energy and a belief in the transformative power of the poetic word. Spiritual and sexual, earthy and refined, a woman's voice speaks to women and to the feminine in women and men – of an openness to life, a surrender to the workings of love, and a trust in the Dark Goddesses and their ways of leading us through the dance.

'Potent, seminal, visionary' *Kevin George Brown*

Poetry/Dance ISBN 978-1906900-12-0 £9.99

Places of Truth: journeys into sacred wilderness

Jay Ramsay

Poet and psychotherapist Jay Ramsay has been drawn to wild places all his writing life, in search of a particular deep listening experience. 'Trwyn Meditations', a sequence set in Snowdonia, begins this 24-year odyssey. 'By the Shores of Loch Awe' takes us to the fecund wilds of Scotland. 'The Oak' celebrates an ancient tree in the heart of the Cotswolds. 'The Sacred Way' is an evocation of Pilgrim Britain. 'Culbone' records the hidden history of the smallest parish church in England in a steep North Somerset valley near where Coleridge wrote 'Kubla Khan'. The final sequences, 'The Mountain' and 'Sinai', takes us beyond, in all senses, touching the places where we find I and Self.

'Beautiful, resonant, real and layered' *Peter Owen Jones*

Poetry ISBN 978-1-906900-40-3 £12.00 Spirit of Place Volume 4

Ditch Vision: essays on poetry, nature, and place

Jeremy Hooker

Ditch Vision is a book of essays on poetry, nature, and place that extends Jeremy Hooker's thinking on subjects that, as a distinguished critic and poet, he has made his life's work. The writers he considers include Edward Thomas, Robert Frost, Robinson Jeffers, Richard Jefferies, John Cowper Powys, Mary Butts, and Frances Bellerby. Through sensitive readings of these and other writers, he discusses differences between British and American writers concerned with nature and spirit of place. The book also includes essays in which he reflects upon the making of his own work as a lyric poet. Written throughout with a poet's feeling for language, *Ditch Vision* is the work of an exploratory writer who seeks to understand the writings he discusses in depth, and to illuminate them for other readers. Hooker explores the 'ground' of poetic vision with reference to its historical and mythological contexts, and in this connection *Ditch Vision* constitutes also a spiritual quest.

Literary Criticism ISBN 978-1906900-51-9 £14.00

Words of Re-enchantment: writings on storytelling, myth, and ecological desire

Anthony Nanson

The time-honoured art of storytelling – ancestor of all narrative media – is finding new pathways of relevance in education, consciousness-raising, and the journey of transformation. Storytellers are reinterpreting ancient myths and communicating the new stories we need in our challenging times. This book brings together the best of Anthony Nanson's incisive writings about the ways that story can re-enchant our lives and the world we live in. Grounded in his practice as a storyteller, the essays range from the myths of Arthur, Arcadia, and the voyage west, to true tales of the past, science-fiction visions of the future, and the big questions of politics and spirituality such stories raise. The book contains full texts of exemplar stories and will stimulate the thinking of anyone interested in storytelling or in the use of myth in fiction and film.

'This excellent book is written with a storyteller's cadence and understanding of language. Passionate, fascinating and wise.' *Hamish Fyfe*

Storytelling/Mythology/Environment ISBN 978-1-906900-15-1 £9.99

www.ingramcontent.com/pod-product-compliance
Lightning Source LLC
Chambersburg PA
CBHW031616160426
43196CB00006B/159
* 9 7 8 1 9 0 6 9 0 0 4 2 7 *